MW00770781

CONTENTS

SHIV-PURAN

B.K. Chaturvedi

DIAMOND BOOKS

© Publisher

ISBN : 81-7182-721-7

Publisher	: **Diamond Pocket Books (P) Ltd.**
	X-30, Okhla Industrial Area, Phase-II
	New Delhi-110020
Phone	: 011-41611861
Fax	: 011-41611866
E-mail	: sales@diamondpublication.com
Website	: www.diamondpublication.com
Edition	: 2006
Price	: 95.00
Printer	: Aadarsh Printers,
	Navin Shahdara, Delhi- 32

Shiv Purana   Rs. 95/-
By : B.K. Chaturvedi

Preface

Needless to emphasies that the Shiv Purana comprises the most authentic details about Lord Shiva. The whole treatise on ancient knowledge has been converted into small stories in this book for easy comprehensions of our readers. Most of the details which are repititive and already mentioned in our 'Vishnu Purana' have been briefly recounted for saving on space. At times there appeared some confusion about the details which have been hinted in the footnotes. Since most of these stories are allegorical in genre, their true significance has also been suggested with in the parenthesis. In short, what you have in your hands is an essential translation cum explanation of the Shiv Purana. It has been done precisely for two reasons. One to make the comprehension logical and secondly to skip the other ritualistic details which may not be found useful for our lay-readers. The attempt is to give a brief but comprehensive glimpse into this Purana to our readers and inspire them to be more versed inferring those roots that form our psyche and evolve our religio cultural ethos.

It is hoped that this second flower of our bouquet of the Puranas will also be accorded a warm welcome. Lastly the author wishes to convey his gratitude to **Narendraji** of *Diamond Publications* whose enthusiasm to revive our culture knows no bounds. Hats off to such 'Atlases' !

—*B. K. Chaturvedi*

1.

Shiv Purana : An Introduction

Although it is doubtful whether the 'Shiva-Purana'is a 'Mahapurana'or not, since at times, the Mahapurans' list includes the Vayu purana also instead of the 'Shiv Purana', there is no doubt it is an important treatise on the deity whose popularity defer any kind of classifications. Because, among the Hindu Supreme Dieties, Viz. Vishnu, Shiv and Brahma, it is only Shiv who is adorable by all category of beings. He is worshipped by the demons and hearts alike apart from being an adorable Lord for the gods and humans. He is the only Lord who doesn't distinguish his devotees according to the species they belong to, but only by feeling of devotion and faith. That is the reason perhaps most of the deadly demon like Ravana etc.had received the boons from only Shiva.

In fact the ancient sages had divided all the eighteen Puranas in to three broad categories and each group has six texts. The Hindu trinity consists of Brahma, Vishnu and Mahesh (Shiv) . Brahma is regarded as the creator, Vishnu the preserver and Shiv the destroyer of the creations. Since all three are important gods, all three are given due emphasis in any Purana. However, the relative emphasis keeps on varying from Purana to Purana. Texts which talk a lot about the various incarnations of the Surpreme Deity (Vishnu) are called 'Satavika' Puranas. Texts which lay emphasis on creation give more importance to Brahma and are called 'Rajasika' Puranas. And those that lay emphasis on the destructive aspect of the Supreme Lord are called 'Tamasika' Puranas. Thus the Shiv Purana is very much of the third category. Other Puranas in this category are the Matsya Purana, the Karma Purana, the Linga Sikanda and Agni Purana. All these Puranas enshrine the records of creation since its very inceptions, with the text varying in emphasis according to the aspect of creations being emphasised.

The Shiv Purana is a much sacred text for the Hindus, particularly to those that adhere on Shiv's faith and are called 'Shaiva'. This is a huge tome containing 24,000 Shlokas. They are divided into six 'Samhitas' (Pandicts or sections). The names of these 'Samhitas', are 'Gyan Samhita' 'Vidyeshwar Samhita' 'Kailash Samhita' 'Sanat-Kumar Samhita', 'Vayaviya Samhita' and 'Dharma Samhita'. Each 'Samhita' is further divided into chapters called the adhyaya. While the 'Gyan Samhita has seventy-eight chapters, 'Vidyeshwar Samhita' Sixteen, 'Kailash Samhita' twelve, Sanat-Kumar Samhita fifty-nine, 'Vayaviya samhita, thirty and the 'Dharma Samhita' sixty nine.

All these Puranas were compiled and edited by Vedyas and his disciple Romaharshana or Lomaharshana recite his Shiv Purana before the seers and sages to emphases the supreme importance of Lord Shiv.

As hinted earlier, Lord Shiv is trully the deity of all those who have no other succour or promise of help from any other deities. That is the reason why his worship is so easy. He could be pacified or glatifie by a mere root or flower, unlike Lord Vishnu's worship which requires costly and eleborate rituals. What is of supreme importance in Shiva's worship is the purity of feeling. Being the incharge of destruction, he is very much capable of deferring the destruction should he get pleased. That is the reason behind his extreme popularity. Now we shall be discussing as to what the sage Lomaharshana told the seers and sages about this most popular Hindu deity.

❑❑

2.

Thus Spake Lomaharshana

Nensisharanya is a place near modern Lucknow which was a very holy spot in ancient times. Owing to the place where the ancestor of Raja Janaka (of Ramayana fame) had performed holy Yagya, it became all the more hallow, and the favourite spot of the seer's assembly. This was the place where eons ago many renound sages dwelt.

One day these sages accosted Lomaharshana[1] and requested:

"O great sage ! Yours is a blessed existence since your acquired knowledge in sucriptures from the very foremost of them, the sage Vedavayas'. Hence there is nothing under the sun that is not within your ken. You can see the past, present and future as clearly of this entire world as though it be a fruit lying on the back of your palm. We requet you to enlighten about Lord Shiva's glory as we are all very eager to know it."

Lomahharshana replied : "Very well sages. Many years ago the sage Narada had expressed this desire before Lord Brahma, the creator, and whatever he told him shall now he narrated by me."

□□

---

1. Literally meaning some one who is ever as thrilled as to make his hair stand on their end.

3.
The Story of Brahma

The universe was a huge naught at the beginning of the creations. It is said that there was only Brahman (the Supreme Essence) that was everywhere . Then there was nothing hot and cold, thick or thin, subtle or manifest. There was water every where. Lord Vishnu manifested himself in his great form, and slept on the water to earn the epithet 'Narayan' for himself. While Vishnu was asleep, a lotus flower (Padma) sprouted out of his navel. It had uncountable petels and its stem glittred as through it was radiated by a million shines. It was from the cells of that lotus that Brahma was born. As he become conscious of his existence he was bewildered and began to wonder:

"Doesn't here exist anything else than this lotus which seems to permeate everywhere.

And then he began to ask himself.

"Who am I and where from have I originated? Who am I? What is the porpose of my existence?"

Not getting replies to the queries that kept on distrubing his mimd, he thought he might get the answer to the quiries if he explored the unending lotus.

"Maybe I get a clue about my existence?"

With this thought upper most in his mind Brahma descended down the stem of the lotus and wandered around for about a hundred years. However no matter what efforts he made he could neither find the centre or beginning or end of the huge lotus flower. Then he decided that he might as well go back to the cell from where he had been born. But despite his roaming about here and there all around the lotus he failed to find the cell from which he originated. This he had kept on doing so for another 100 years. Now he was so much exhausted in his effort that he decided to give up the search and rested.

All of a sudden, he heard a loud voice commanding him:

"Brahma , perform tapasya (meditation) and be calm,"

Following the command Brahma meditated for twelve years. When that period was drawing to a close, there appeared Lord Vishnu in his four-armed form before a bewildered Brahma. Vishnu had in his four hands a 'Shankha' (couch-shell) 'Chakra' (a sharp bladid discus), a gada (mace) and a flower of lotus called Padma. Brahma was non-pleased to see this strange form and out of his curiosity he asked:

"Who are you, Lord?

Vishnu evaded a direct answer to this question and replied:

"Son ! You have been created by Lord Vishnu?"

"But who are you to address me as 'son'? demanded Brahma rather peevishly.

"Can't you recognise me, son," asked Vishnu.

"I'm Vishnu and I sired you from my body from which you have originated."

But Brahma was not at all convinced. Since Vishnu couldn't produce the evidence to substantiate his claim, Brahma took unbrage on his calling him his son. With the result, he began to fight with Vishnu.

The Appearnce of the Linga

While they were engaged in a close fight, there apeared a shining column called the Linga. It was so huge that it seemed to have no beginning or the end.

Where upon Brahma was advised by Vishnu : "Let us stop fighting since we also have a third being amidst us. Let us first try to know about this linga. What on earth is this column? What is its origin or where and how has it appeared here as if from no where? Brahma, having ended his fruitless search too measure the lotus already, was not to enthusiastic to learn about this linga.

Then Vishnu advised again. "You adopt the form of a swan (Hansa) and go up and I shall adopt the form of a Boar (Varaha) to go down. Let us try and explore to the extremities of this huge column, called linga."

Brahma didn't objected to the suggestion. Adopting the form of a white swan he flew up. Vishnu took the form of a white boar and went down. They both remained engrossed in their search for four thousand

11

years but couldn't reach the end of that linga. None of them could get to the either extremity of that endless object. At last they returned to where they had started off from and began to pray. For about a thousand years they continued to pray. It was when that big period was coming to a close that they heard the sound of 'OM'. Along with that sound a being with five faces and ten arms appeared before them. That was Mahadeva or Shiv in his original form.

Vishnu bowed to that great existence and quipped:

"It is good that Brahma and I have been fighting which has seemingly brought you here."

Shiv replied soberly : "Be not confused. We are all three parts of the same entity. We are one and the same though having different forms. While Brahma is the creator, Vishnu is the preserver, I am the destroyer. These are the roles that Supreme Entity has assigned to us. There is another being named Rudra who will originate from my body. But understand that Rudra and I will not be different. In fact we all are one and the same. Now let Brahma start his role as the creator."

Thus enlighted, Vishnu and Brahma gave up their forms of a swan and a boar and Shiv disappeared as his two associates regained their original form.

| In yet another mythological account it is said that in searching the extremities of that Linga, Brahma took recourse to fakehood to claim his getting to the end of the linga. In his support he had brought a flower of ketaki also which he claimed he found. It was then that Shiv cursed Brahma that since he spoke untruth he would not get his due worship from the beings and forbade the use of ketaki flower in his worship.|

□□

12

4.

Brahma Begins the process of Creation

In the beginning there was water everywhere . In the water, Vishnu created a huge egg (the Anda). He then himself entered the egg. Since Brahma was born of that Golden egg he is often called Hiranyagarbha.

In the meantime, Brahma, after his own creation was asked to meditate. From the powers of his meditation he created several sages (Rishis). Kardam, Daksha and Mareechi were among them. Mareechi's son was kashyapa. Daksha had sixty daughters and he married thirty of them to Kashyapa. Out of this wedlock it was kashyapa who can be literally called the sire of creation as all the gods (called Aditya since their mother was Aditi), demons (called Daitya because their mother was Diti), Danavas trees, birds, snakes, mountains, and creepers populated the world.

One day Brahma was asked by the sages (divine Rishis) in the presence of Vishnu as to who was the greatest among the Trinity. Brahma, Shiv or Vishnu. Brahma declared that he was, where upon a dispute arose between Brahma and Vishnu. At length they agreed to refer the matter to the authority of the Vedas. The sacred books declared that this honour belonged to Shiv.

The other two protested, "how can the Lord of goblins, the delighter in grave yards, wearing twisted locks ornamented by snakes, be supreme?" Even as they said this, Shiv sprang into their midst in human form, vast and terrible. On seeing him the fifth head of Brahma glowed with anger and said: "I know thee will, O Chandrashekhar[1], for from my forehead didst thou spring, and because those didst weep I called thee Rudra[2]. Hasten then to seek the refuge of my feet, and I will protect thee, O my son !"

---

1. Literally meaning one who wears moon at his crown of head.
2. Literally meaning one who weeps.

At these proud words Shiv was incensed who instantly cut off the head of Brahma with the thumb nail of Bhairava's left hand.

Rudra, Shiv's another form, lived on Mount Kailash. Daksha's daughter, Sati, was married to Rudra (Shiv)

However, Shiv and Daksha did not have good terms. Once in Brahma's assembly, when Shiv entered all the major and minor gods stood up in reverence barring Daksha who thought that since Shiv was his son-in-law, he should not command any respect from him. Much later on, Daksha was declared Prajapati (Progenitor) by Brahma and to celebrate this occasion he arranged for a massive 'Yagya' (sacrifice) in which he extended invitations to all gods barring his son-in-law, Shiv due to old vancour. Although Sati was not invited either yet despite Shiva's counter counsel she went to attend the function at her father's place uninvited. But when she saw that oblation for every major or minor god was assigned and there was no such offering for her lord and one of the major deity of the Supreme trinity, she was so upset by this blatant contempt shown by her father that she decided to end her life by jumping into the holy pit of the yagya's fire. Her ire had been further aggravated by her father also showing utter contempt to her as well. When Shiv (Rudra) heard about the happening at the yagya venue and his wife's death under protest, he was so much angered that he sent his hench persons led by Veer Bhadra to destroy the whole ceremony and kill all the gods who had gone to attend it. This was done but Rudra who was still not pacified. Extracting the body of Sati from the holy pit he began to dance his Tandava Dance while keeping Sati's body slung across his sholder. Subsequently Vishnu, on the request of other gods who feared that the whole earth world slide to Patal if Shiv continued to act in such a berserk manner cut the body of Sati into many pieces. When that died head was gone, Shiv's anger was pacified and with his permission the gods slain at the sacrifice were revived to life and the incomplete sacrifice was duly completed.

Sati, being immensely attached to Shiv, was reborn as the daughter of the mountain king Himalaya (Himvant), and his queen Maina. In this life, Sati's name was Parvati.

Although Shiv, after Sati's death had become a total ascetic and he had no interest left to remarry, the circumstance developed in such a way that eventually with the consent and design of the gods and high seens he agreed to marry Parvati.

❏❏

5.

The Story of Tarakasura

There was a mighty Asura (demon) named Tara. After some time he got a son who was as determined and powerful as his father had been, He knew that unless he developed some extra powers through a divine boon he would never be able to defeat his arch rivals, the gods.

With this resolve he decided to perform a severe penance to please the creator. He therefore, repaired the holy places called Madhuvana and begn to perform his difficult 'Tapasya' to achieve his aim. He continuously gazed at the sun and stood there for years with his both arms raised heavenwards, as if beckoning at the heaven to said Brahma. Then he stood for many years on one leg and then on the toes of his feet. A hundred years passed but Brahma didn't appear before him. For those 100 years Taraka drank only water and didn't eat even a morsel of food. For the next 100 years, he gave up that too and survived on inhibiting air only. Then he performed his penance for another 100 years inside water, another 100 years on earth under most difficult conditions and yet another 100 years even inside fire. When Brahma was not yet pleased for another 100 years the demon performed his 'tapasya' upside down, standing on his bare hands. Then he locked his feet to a sturdy branch and hanged himself for another 100 years this way.

Seeing the determination of Taraka, Brahma could no longer postpone his apperance before the demon-lord, Eventually he revealed himself near Taraka and said:

"Get up, son ! I'm pleased with your Tapasya. What boon do you seek from me."

"O Lord !" Taraka replied, "if you are really pleased with me then grant me two boons. The first boon should be that no one created by you should be as strong as I am. The second boon that I desire is that I should be killed only by Shiva's son!'

Taraka knew that Shiv had no wife at that point of time and that he was quite averse to marrying for the second time, he demanded this boon to ensure his demon's race's eternal rule over the gods.

Brahma, bound by the rule of nature had to grant the boon whoever did so, So he said:

"So be it!" and departed back to his realm. Mightily pleased at his achieving the desired boon the demon lord returned to his capital called Shonitpur and began to gather army to defeat the gods. Mean while, all the members of the demon race, upon hearing Taraka's splendid achievement , made him the role leader of the entire demon race. The boon, enhanced his power as much as to face no obstruction in achieving his aim and in no time he defeated the gods and thrown them out of their capital. He then conquered all the three worlds and drove the gods out of heaven. He snatched all their priced belongings and put them in his employment with torturous conditions.

Those of them that managed to escape reached Brahma in utter despondent state and recountered the horrors they had to suffer because of Taraka's tyranny. "O creator! please help us and solve this problem. Taraka is so powerful that we may, perhaps, never be able to defeat him. Will we ever get to our old glorious position and recapture our lost heaven ?"

"The problem can't be solved immediately' replied Brahma thoughtfully.

"According to the boon I have given to him, he can be killed only by Lord Shiv's son. But Shiv, at present, has no wife, let alone a son. He has got to be propitiated so that he gives his consent for second marriage. The girl fit to be his wife has already taken birth. Now he is performing meditations at Kailash and the girl, named Parvati, is also doing her penance to rejoin Shiv as her husband. You must do some thing to see that Shiv marries her. Engender a desire for a wife in his heart."

The gods returned to their hiding place, thinking over what they should do to make Shiv accept Parvati as his wife.

❏❏

6.

Kama Deva, the Love god Incinerated

Following Brahma's advice the gods went to Indra, their leader and told him all that Brahma had advised them. Indra at once summoned Kamadeva (also called Kanderpa or Madana) and said. "My friend, you will have to come to our rescue. Since only you can engender the longing for physical union in any body's heart There is no way but your going straight to Shiv meditating on Kailash with your entire love inducing paraphernalia. Kindle the feeling of love in him so that he may give his consent for second marriage. Make sure that Shiv and Parvati fall in each other's love. This you will have to do else we may never return to heaven!"

Getting this challanging assignment kanderpa was a bit nervous. He thought, 'Shiv is a mighty lord endowed with a fiery sight. Even if I get burnt in his anger, I would have proved my worth in the Goddom" So taking along his wife, Rati, his friend, spring and his soft bow shooting flower laden arrows, he reached near Kailash and hid himself behind a bush. And as soon as the god of love apeared on the mount, the place took on the traits of a speing which was perennial. Flowers bloomed, trees oozed their green felicity and bees buzzed around the flowers. Cuckoos sang and fragrant Zephyrs started blowing every where nature appeared as comely as to make even the inamimate object long for embrace and kisses. Shiv was also some what distracted. Though he tried to concentrate on his meditation, he couldn't get it instantly. In this disturbance Shiv opened his eyes for once and beheld Kama hiding behind a flowery bush with his bow shooting an arrow of flower which struck Shiv at the heart region 'So it is Kama who is behind all this disturbance and the unusual advent of the spring season !' Thus angered, Shiv opened his third eye which was in the middle of his forehead. Out emerged from that eye a strong beem of dazzling light which incinerated Kama instantly. At once Rati, the wife of Kama cried for help. Hearing her voice filled with supplication, Shiv said : "Since your husband had tried to disturb my equipoise, I burnt him down. But pleaded by your prayer I grant him this boon that even though his body is burnt, he has not died and may live through the feeling of love. In Dwapar yg when Krishna will get a son called Pradyumna in his body Kama will regain his body, Now you return with you husband's spirit (soul) and let me meditate."

But despite being physically burnt to ashes, Kama had done his job. Now Shiv, bitten by the love-bug, started seeing in his mental yision a beautiful girl who was none other than Parvati.

☐☐

7.
Parvati's Birth Legend

As has been hinted before, Parvati was the reincarnation of Sati. Sati had immolated herself in the holy-fire at her father's yagya. But even before that Shiv had mentally rejected her as his wife. The detailed story is as follows.

Way back in the Treta Yug, Once Shiv and Sati went to sage Agastya's hermitage where the story of Rama's doing was being recited. They sat quietly and listened to that most absorbing story along with other listeners. The sage Agastya told the story in such a spell-binding way that Sati felt as though she was visually beholding Rama, Sita, Lakshaman and other persons before her eyes. After some time when the recitation was over, the couple left for Kailash. But Shiv kept quite, and appeared still lost in that enchanting tale. Although Sati had tried to ask a few questions to distract him, he remained mostly reticent and incommunicative.

All of a sudden Sati beheld her lord, Shiv, bowing before two ascetic-like persons moving far away from them, "Who they could be to command so reverent a greeting from supreme Lord Shankar?" Sati wondered "Could they be Rama and Lakshamana?" She knew that by that time only Vishnu's Rama incarnation had taken place but even Sita had been abducted. "And even though one of them be Rama the incarnation of Lord Vishnu, my Lord is also as venerable as Vishnu is. Then why this extra reverential bowing?" These throughts kept disturbing Sati's mind. At last, when she couldn't find any logical answer she asked her lord, Shankar: " Lord ! why must be so respectful to a mortal king's son? Shiv corrected her. "No, he is not only the mortal king's son but the incarnation of my chosen deity, Lord Vishnu !"

19

"I knew it," said Sati, "Still it doesn't satisfy my query. If he is Supreme Lord Vishnu, he knows that what ever he has been doing is a mortal play for he knows that he would win back his lost wife. When he knows everything, the beginning and end of everything, why must he pretend so much grief and unnecessarily make his devoted brother Lakshman also sad. In fact all these contradictions raise some doubt about his reality."

At this, Shiv became rather serious and said "I told you, he is Vishnu in the mortal form. If you have any doubt, well, test him to satisfy your curiosity. Meanwhile, I'll wait beneath this banyan tree. When you return, you will find me here only."

Saying so, Shiva kept quiet, now Sati was in a fix. She had detected a touch of asperity in her lord's voice. He appeared rather angry to her. Now if she went back to him with the plea that she had no doubt, he was sure to realise that she was telling a blatant lie. Then she reasoned in her mind : "I think there is no harm in my testing Ram whether he is only the mortal king's son or the incarnation of Vishnu as well. In case he is my lord's chosen deity and the Supreme Lord, certainly his 'darshan' would cause me no harm. On the contrary, seeing the Supreme Lord I would be all the more blessed. And in case he is not Lord Vishnu's mortal form and only the son of a mortal king, then I'd have proved my doubt to be well substantiated. May be, through this test my lord wants to test my faith in him as well. I must go ahead and do the test." With this thought and resolve upper most in her mind, she advanced towards the direction she had seen the two brothers going in.

But she also realised that she had devised no plan to conduct the test to identify the reality. Then she hit upon a brilliant ieda. "He is becoming so mad with seperation of his wife that he is indiscriminately inquiring even from the creepers, trees and mountains whether they had seen his wife. So the best way to test Rama is to reach before him in Sita's disguise. If he is a mortal being he would fall into that trap. But if he is really the Divine Lord, he would see through my disguise and know the reality.

Then she disguised herself as Sita, recollecting the details of her beauty by the sage Agastya's description that she had heard about only recently. So with great patience she adopted Sita's form and reached suddenly before the two wandering brothers. Lakshaman was amazed to see 'Sita' before him. With disbelief he looked at his elder brother, Rama, who was smiling. Immidiately Rama bowed his head to her and asked her: "O Great Goddess ! Why are you loitering in this forest all alone ? Where is my Chosen deity, Lord Shankar?"

As Rama pronounced Shankar's name all doubts in her mind were instantly cleared and she was now convinced that Rama was not only the son of a renowned mortal dynasty but the incarnation of the Blessed Lord Vishnu himself. Leaving Rama's question unanswered-'the Supreme Lord knows every secret' - she rushed back to that banyan where her lord was waiting for her.

Meanwhile, by his divine powers Shiv had seen all that Sati did before Rama, Since he treated Sita almost like his mother, he decided to leave Sati for good as his wife because he couldn't have accepted some one like a mother to him as his wife.

But when Sati returned and Shiv asked as to how did she performes the test. She tried to evade the question by saying the test eventually wasn't needed as she believed to be true all-that he had said earlier. But Shiv knew the reality yet kept mum, However, Sati also detected some change in his behaviour to her. The most blatant was when on her return, Shiv asked her to sit before him and not at her traditional position, on the left of her husband. This and other subsequent marked changes in Shiv's behaviour communicated a clear message to Sati that Shiv no more treated her as his wife. Sati was deeply hurt at Shiv's this decision. She often wondered that why only a temporary change of her appearance deprived her of her permanent position. But Shiv's decision was final and firm. Thenceforth despite being descented by her husband Sati had to suffer the agony to stay with her husband and pretend to the outside world as through no change had occured in their relationship. It was a very painful living for her and mentally she started praying to almighty that she be given an oportunity to escape this mental torture.

That opportunity was provided by the way that her father was organising a massive yagya to celebrate his becoming the progenitor of the world. There she reached uninvited and finding her husband insulted by her father, ended her life by jumping into the holy-pit of fire.

It was only then that the demon lord Taraka had started troubling the gods who designed for Shiv's second marriage so-that the Lord (Shiv) could produce the slayer of Taraka, as Brahma had ordained. In the attempt to make Shiv ready for his second marriage Kama had to sacrifies his body.

Kama or Kandarpa's wife was Rati. When Rati saw that her husband had been burnt to ashes, her grief knew no bounds. At last, she lost consciousness. When she recovered, she lamented. "Who is me. Now What is going to happen to me? My husband, my love-where are you?"

The gods felt pity at Rati's condition. They took her to Shiv. When he learnt about the whole happening he said : "Well, what was destined has happened. Nothing can be done about Kandarpa now. But he will eventually be born in the city of Dwarika in Krishna's son Pradyumna. Then only Rati will be united with Kama. But till such time, let her simply wait.

Although the gods returned with Rati, they were quite despondant. Instead of getting Shiv's consent for second marriage, they had lost the body of one of their beloved collieagues.

□□

22

8.
Parvati's Great Penance

But all this while, Parvati continued to be drawn towards Shiv. The more she heard about him the more she liked him. She had also learnt from her maid that the divine Sage Narada had predicted that she was destined to get only Shiv as her husband, How it happened is given in details below.

After the death of Sati, she was reborn as the daughter of the Himalaya king named Himvant and his wife Maina. As the providence world have it, a few days after Parvati or Uma's birth, the divine Sage Narada happened to visit their kingdom. After respectfully welcoming him the king said with the folded hands : "O Divine Sage! You have access to every part of the universe and you know about everybeing's past, present and future. Would you please be kind enough to tell about my daughter's future."

The divine sage then saw the horoscope and palm of that child daughter and said: "O Kind ! Your daghter is an extremely blessed existence. She will become the model of all women of the world as far as their conjugal happeniness is concerned. She will enjoy an eternal, blessed married life. Her husband will be a renowned and highly adorable person. But, "the sage paused for a few seconds which made the girl's parents very anxious . The king hurriedly asked : "But, what—? sage ?"

"She is destined to have some one as her husband who shall he homeless, scantily dressed, fond of all kind of narcotic drugs and whose ornaments would be snakes and his body would be dressed with the ash of the died bodies."

Hearing this, Maina, the girl's mothed was very nervous. The king was also crest-fallen having heard with great glee the first part of the prediction. He again asked : "Sage ! what are you saying ? The sage replied: "Worry not O king! All these attributes that I have described fit only Shankar, the Blessed Lord ! so by logic it is apparent that her husband would be no one else but Lord Shankar himself!"

Although the divine sage's explanation pacified the king, Maina was still not reconciled. It was only when the king explained to her that they were very fortunate to get Lord Shankar as the son-in-law that the royal lady was somewhat normal.

When Parvati heard about this prediction she was besides herself with joy. Right from the day she became concious she had her mind fixed on Lord Shankar.

One day the sage Narada came again and told her, "Shiv is only pleased with dedicated penance. In fact without deep concentration even Brahma and other gods are deprived of Lord Shiv's 'Darshan'. So, if you want Shiv you must perform 'Tapasya'.

Parvati decided to do exactly what Narada had advised her. She asked parents for permission. Her father agreed with alacrity. Although her mother Maina was not at all keen that Parvati should perform so difficult Tapasya, she too eventually agreed. Discending her royal clothes and ornaments, she immediately wore deer skin instead. Then she returned to the peak[1] in the Himalayas. Reaching there she started her meditation and making it more and more difficult. First she left food, then water and then started serviving only on inhibiting air. She had looked so weak that she acquired the epithet 'Aparna' which literally meanes a leaf-less tree. During rains she meditated on the ground undaunted by constant shower and in winters she started meditating even under water. Although the place was lonely with few wild beasts also available there, she remanied fearless. Even the beasts dared not harm her. Her concentration and dedication was so strong that all the gods and sages assembled there to witness this unprecedented 'Tapasya' by a mere girl.

Seeing the girl's firmness of resolve to have Lord Shiv as her husband, the gods and sages also began to pray to Shiv. "O Lord !

---

1. **Now called Gauri Shikhar; it is a peak named so since Gauri (Parvati) had performed her tapasya there.**

Parvati is performig a very difficult penance. No one has meditated with this kind of dedication like this before. Please grant her whatever she wants."

Then Shiv selected a team of wise sages and asked them to dissuade her from her firm resolve in order to test her faith in Him.'

The sages adopted the form of old brahmans and appeared before Parvati. "O girl ! What for you are performing such a dedicated meditation. What is that you want to achieve by so severely torturing your comely and lithe body ?"

Parvati duly welcomed them and offered choicest fruits to them. Then coyly she said : "O lords of the earth ! I want to have Shiv as my husband !"

"You are indeed stupid," they said with a touch of asperity in their voice "You are as much insane as to pray for wine against the possibility of having nectar or ask for mud against sandalwood. Would any one go for inhibing well-water if one has the Ganga flowing before him. Why must you opt for Shiv, a homeless ascetic addicted to all sort of narcotic drugs and moving about dishevelled and dirty in a wild company of ghosts and goblins ? Marry one of the gods instead. Indra and Vishnu are the ideal choice for any girl. Shiv is not a good choice. He keeps his body smeared with the ashes of crematoriums and has poison in his throat that has turned it blue. We all think that you are committing a big mistake by praying to get him as your husband. Forget Shiv or your whole life will be wasted. A girl like you very much deserves a handsome god like Vishnu. If you want we may ask him to accept you as his bride."

The brahmanas' words greatly angered Parvati who couldn't hide her indignation and blurted out: "Perhaps you won't mind my saying but the fact is that it is the persons like you who are stupid."

She continued : "I am amazed that despite your appearing so learned you betray your crass ignorance. You yourselves don't know anything about Shiv. He is the lord of all beings of the universe. The only one to care for the distressed and down-trodden. It is to keep this world pure and pions that he drank the poison. He is the only lord to be won not by flamboyant riches but purity of feeling. You have not only insulted Shiv but have commited a sin by voicing such obsecne words about him. How foolish I have been to welcome such a bunch of silly fellows. Now, before you say anything nasty about him, allow me to go away. I can't stand Shiv's calumniators. I must get away before you say anything foul about my chosen lord."

As Parvati was about to get away the brahmans smiled and said. "Don't go away, O determined girl ! We came here only to test your faith in your chosen lord, at his bidding only. Now we bless you that you shall have him only as your husband."

So saying the brahmans departed and told Shiv about Parvati. Shiv was delighted to know about Parvati's so deep love for him. Then he finally consented for his marriage to Parvati. The gods were overjoyed and they began to make preparation for that grand marriage. Now they had crossed the first hurdle in realising their ambition of making Lord Shiv's son kill the demon Taraka.

❑❑

9.

Lord Shiv's Marriage To Parvati

S hiv called the seven great sages (the saptarishis) and asked
them to go to the father of Parvati with a proposal from his
side in a formal way. The king Himavant was delighted to receive
the offer and more delighted to see the divine sage Narada's prediction
was coming true. To have the lord of universe as is son-in-low was a
big feather to his cap. He readily consented and cousulted his
astrologers to find a suitable day for his daughter's marriage. The
day eventually chosen was the 'Triyodashi' or the thirteenth day of
the waning moon (dark) fortnight of the month of Phalguna. (Mid
Feb to Mid March)

Soon the day of the marriage dawned. Gandharvas (the divine
singers) sang and the Apsaras (the divine dancers) danced, making
the entire Nature pleased and joyfull. All the gods riding their vehicles
rushed to Kailash to accompany Shiv in the procession of his marriage.
This was a most unusual marriage party which had very varied
members. While on one side were the celestials glittering in their
divine apparels and ornaments, on the other, were the most dreadful
ghosts, goblins, beasts, demons who also walked behind the unique
groom clad in his deerskin and decorated by snakes and ash . The
king Himavant also got ready to welcome the 'Barata' (marriage-
party). He had built many gates in front of his palace and had placed
small flags on them. So beutiful those arched and flagged gates looked
that time that even the thousand-hooded serpent, Shesh, or the goddess
of speech, Sharada, couldn't have described their grandeur and
comeliness. When the huge procession having beings of every species
reached close to the palace, Maina, Parvati's mother, rushed out to

accord the formal welcome to the groom. She was thinking that the groom, for which her daughter had performed so difficult a penance must be a person of outstanding handsomewomen. But she was in for many surprises.

The first person she saw was Vishwavasu, the kind of the gandharvas. He was very handsome and, at first, Maina throught that this was Shiv. But when she was told that this was only a singer who entertained Shiv, she thought that Shiv would be more handsome. Then her eyes fell on a handsome Kubera, the custodian of all divine wealth, but she was told that neither he was Shiv. This way her eyes kept on searching the progressively handsome Yama, Varuna, Surya, Chandra but each time Narada told her that none of them was Shiv but her potential son-in-low's attendants. Nevertheless, Maina was besides herself looking at these 'servants', thinking that if the mere attendants were so handsome, how handsome would be their master. Again, she mistook Brahma, Vishnu and Vrahaspati but Narada told her that neither of them was Shiv. Now Maina's curiosity knew no bounds. 'After all, where is the groom, Shiv', she wondered. Finally Shiv came and Narada pointed out to Maina. But as she beheld her potential son-in-low she fell unconscious in the mere shock of what she expected and what she actually saw.

For the groom, Shiv, was surrounded by ghosts on all sides. Their faces were fierce, their complexions dark and eerie and they formed an apparently very vicious group. Shiv himself was riding a bull. He was in his full form: three eyes, five faces and many arms. He was smeared with ashes and the moon adorned his forehead. He was clad in a tiger's skin and a garland of skulls being around his neck. It was his this form beholding which Maina had fainted.

When she recovered, she began to lament and curse Narada. "What harm did I caused him to make him select this deadly looking person as the groom for my darling daughter. "She scolded the king Himavanta and Parvati for falling into the trap laid by Narada. Bewailing loudly our her misfortune she retired back to her palace. Brahma and other gods and the sages tried their best to pacify Maina but to no avail.

"I won't permit my daughter to marry this eerie-looking person," she thundered. "Instead, I would prefer to consume poison and kill my daughter also but till I am here this marriage shall not take place." She announced with a touch of finality. Then Parvati came forward herself to resolve the impasse. "The earth may be torn to pieces and the ocean may dry but I shall not marry anyone else except Shiv. Could a jackal be a fit replacement for a lion?"

Then Vishnu came forward to pacify Maina and resolve the matter. But he did not succeed either. Finally Narada requested Shiv to display his beautiful form and Shiv obliged. This form is exhibited to only those who are very faithful to Shiva. Everyone present there was instantly charmed by his beautiful form including Maina. His body shone like a thousand suns and a crown sparkled on his head. His clothes glittered and the lustrre of his jewels put the stars to shame.

Now it was Maina's turn to be apologetic to Shiva. She begged forgiveness and now there were no further obstacles to the marriage. Then, under the supervision of Brahma, the marriage ceremony was gone through with full gaiety and grandeur. Thus united in the wedlock, Shiv and Parvati repaired to Kailash. The gods were delighted to have crossed the second hurdle towards realization of their aim : the birth of a son to Shiv to slay the deadly demon Taraka. Praising Shiv and Parvati they repaired to their respective realms.

□□

10.

The Tale Relating to Birth of Kartikeya

Shiv and Parvati remained for many years in Kailash and eventually they produced a beautiful son. He was named Kartikeya. Why this name, literally meaning 'of the Krittikas', was given has a legend woven inside it.

When the baby was born and still in his infancy, he was lost in some reeds. Closely living were six krittikas (also called a kind of princess but/they were allegorically the six seasons) who discovered this boy. Now each of them wanted to feed this boy by their divine powers. They made the boy develop six faces. Hence one of the epithet of Kartikeya is 'Shada - anana' which literally means some one having six faces. They then raised the boy up jointly. So the boy acquired the name Kartikeya.

When the gods heard about Kartikeya's birth, they rejoiced. Now they had some one who could slay their scourge, Tarakasur. As Kartikeya grew up, he emerged as a robust lad, very powerful and deft in all martial arts. The gods then appointed Kartikeya the Commander of the divine forces. Under his leadership the gods attacked the demon Taraka's citadel, Shonitpur.

A terrible fight raged for as many as ten days. But under the able leadership of Kartikeya the gods managed to completely decimate the demons. Eventually Kartikeya killed Tarakasura in a duel. After the demon lord's death, the gods trounced the demon hosts and recaptured heaven. They were delighted to get back their best empire. After the victory celebrations were over, Kartikeya was restored to his parents.

❑❑

11.
Creation And Eventual Destruction of Tripura

Tarakasura, the demon had three sons named vidyunmali, Tarakaksha and Viryavana. When they found that their powerful king and father slain through a conspiracy hatched by the gods, in order to avenge their father's death, they began to perform very difficult Tapasya. For a hundred years they meditated standing only on one leg. Then, for a thousand years they lived on air and meditated. Subsequently they stood on their heads and meditated in this posture for yet another 1000 years. Their aim was to propitiate Brahma and seek a desired boon from him.

Eventually Brahma was propitiated by their Tapasya. He appeared before them and asked them to get the boon of their choice.

"Make us immortal," answered Taraksura's sons.

"This is not possible. Everyone who is born must die. This is a universal low of creation,"the creator explained. "Ask for something else instead."

"Very well, then," said Vidyunmali, Tarakaksha and Vi.yavana." Grant us the following. Let three forts be made. The first one of gold, the second of silver and the third of iron. We will live in these forts for about a 1000 years And then after this period the forts should be united and become one impregnable citadel. Then it should be called Tripura. and we may die only when some one be able to destroy this combined citadel called Tripura with a sigle arrow. Make it our destiny."

Brahma was rather amazed to find them seeking this unusual boon but since he was bound by his commitment to the three demons he granted it.

Then the three demons sought the services of Maya danava, the top architect of the demons, to build the desired forts. They requested Brahma to order Maya danava to fulfill their demand. He did so by making the first fort of gold in heaven, the second fort of silver in the sky and the third one of iron on earth. Tarakaksha got the golden fort, Viryavana the silver one and Vidyunmali the iron one. Each of the forts was as big as a city having many Vimanas (Aerial Vehicles) accomodated in each of them. Now ensconced in these forts the three sons of Tarakasura felt quite powerful. They populated the three forts and began to flourish.

Now, their enhancing power was, as always, an anathema to the gods. They first went to Brahma with their complaint of his abetment in letting the demons enhance their power. But Brahma pleaded his innocence as he was bound by the low of nature. Then the celestials sought Lord Shiv's help. But Shiv said that the demons were doing nothing wrong and as long as this was the case he did not see why the gods should be so bothered. At last the god went to Vishnu who gave them the following piece of advice. "If the demons were doing nothing wrong the gods must plan in such a way as to deviate the demons from their chosen path and make them commit sin. For unless the demon turn sinners, even I (Lord Vishnu) can't cause their downfall ."

Then out of his mysterious powers Lord Vishnu created a man. This man's head was shaven, his clothes faded and he carried a wooenwater pot in his hands. He covered his mouth with a piece of cloth and he approached Vishnu.

"What I have been created for ?" that mysterions man asked.

"Let me explain you," Vishnu replied "I will teach you a religion that is completely against the Vedic norms. You will then get the impression as if there is no swarga (heaven), no 'Naraka' (hell) and both exist only on earth itself. You will believe that rewards and punishment for deeds committed on the earth are not meted out after death. Now go to Tripura and teach demons this religion. You must keep on goading the demons to commit sins so that they be totally dislodged from their rightious path. Then only some action could be planned by us against Tripura."

That mysterious man did exactly what he had been asked to do by Lord Vishnu. He was also supported by four disciples and they together went to a forest near Tripura. There they opened their pseudo hermitage and began to preach the faith as advised by Lord Vishnu. Since they were trained by the Blessed Lord Vishnu hemself, their teachings were proving quite convincing. Soon they had many converts as their followers. Meanwhile, the divine sage Narada was acting as a publicity agent and it was he who first carried the names of advent of a new religion to Vidyunmali.

"King," Narada said, "You have close to your temple a wonderful tteacher who preaches a most original religion. I have never heard any one teaching any faith with such conviction and clarity. In fact, I now stand converted to that faith".

Vidyunmali was impressed because like all noble kings he, too, believed and reposed respect in all that the divine sage said. Soon, following Narada, he, too, was converted to the new faith. And in the course, so did Tarakaksha and Viryavana. With the result the demon gave up respecting the vedas and they ceased to worship all gods and Brahmans. They also grew averse to worshiping the 'Linga' of a symbolical manifestation of Lord Shiva.This news was magnified manifold by the gods. Led by Vishnu other gods then went to Shiv and began to pray to him. When Shiv appeared they told him that the demons had now become evil and hence they should be destroyed pronto. "They have grown as much audacions as to stop even worshipping your symbol, the Linga."

Naturally, Shiv was enraged. In the fit of anger he agreed to destroy the demons along with their citadel, the Tripura. Shiv then summoned Vishkarma and asked him to make a suitable chariot, bow and arrow. The chariot was made entirely out of gold. Brahma himself became the charioteer and the chariot was speedily driven towards Tripura. The other gods also accompanied Shiv with divine weapons.

It was about this time that the stipulated time of a 1000 years was drawing to a close. Hence, soon, the three forts coalesced into a single mighty fort. Deeming the opportune hour arriving Shiv installed a divine weapon called 'Pashupati astra' into his arrow and shoot it at Tripura. The arrow struck at the fort and burst it all up into ashes in a trice.

The gods were delighted at the fall of Tripura and they began to celebrate the occasion with quiet gusto. At that time appeared the shaven headed person and asked as to what he and his assistants were supposed to do now. Then Brahma and Vishnu consulted with each other and then ordered: "You all go and live in desert. You may come back to human civilization in the last phase of the Kaliyug era. Then the faith preached by you will have greater impact upon the listners. Till then you with your companions must lie low." and they did so.

□□

12.

Sita And Ketaki Flower

Romharshana, continuing his narration to the large number of the saints and seers assembled in Nemi sharanya, said: "Lord Shiv is Aashutosha or easily propitiable. Not much paraphernalia of ritual worship is needed to please him. He is won more by spirit than by form. However, Shiv must never be worshipped with a Ketaki (Paudanus) or Champak (Michlia Champaca) flower.

The sages were surprised : "Why ? What is wrong with these flowers? Tell us in details about this mystery."

"I will start first with the Ketaki flower," said Romaharshana and narrated the following story.

When asked by king Dasharatha, Rama's father, Rama, alongwith his wife Sita and brother Lakshman, was passing his days in exile on the banks of the river Phalgu, he received the news about his father passing away, unable to bear separation from him the dearest son. Getting this news Rama started to make preparations to perform the Shraddha[1] of his dead father. He decided to take along his brother Lakshman to procure the necessary ingredients from the nearly village. But, on second thought, he thought it wise to send his brother alone for procuring the necessary items as it wasn't prudent to leave Sita alone, unprotected in that jungle. Lakshman went but didn't return for long. This made Rama worried and after making neccessary arrangement for Sita's security, this time he went to procure the things and trace Lakshman. But Rama too didn't return. It was almost noon

---

1. A ceremony to offer food to brahmans to show our'gratitude to the departed soul.

35

and the ceremony had to be performed before noon. In desperation, Sita herself decided to perform the ceremony with whatever ingredients that were available there. She went and bathed in the river Phalgu. Then she lit an earthen lamp. She then made the offerings (pinda) to offer it to the dead ancestors. When she had almost completed the ceremony she heard a voice emerging from no where but heavens. "Sita, you are blessed, We are satisfied." And in utter amazement she watched some of the disembodied hands appear in the air to accept the offerings.

Bewildered and curious, she asked: "Who are you ? Why don't you come in the open ?" The voiced said : "I'm your dead father-in-low. You have successfully completed the ceremony. I have accepted your offerings."

But your sons, my hushand, and his brother are not going to believe me, "Sita said "They will never believe that such disembodied hands had appeared out of thin air to accept the offerings."

"They have to," responded the voice, "You have four witnesses. The first is the river Phalgu. The scond is the cow over there. The third is the fire and the last will be the Ketaki bush whose flowers you offered with the ceremonial material " Saying so, the died king's hands disappeared along with the voice.

But Sita's apprehension was true. When Rama and Lakshmana returned they said : "Cook the food quickly. There is very little time left for completing the Shraddha."

Then Sita told them all that she had accomplished. But the two brothers refused to believe that Sita had completed the ceremony in their absence. Instead of believing her they made fun of Sita and suggested that she must be lying. Then Sita called upon her four witnesses. But, to her surprise each of them denied having seen anything. Without arguing any further she cooked the food and Rama made the offering to his ancestors.

Suddenly a voice boomed from the sky. "Why are you invoking us again? Sita has already satisfied us."

But Rama was adamant : "I refuse to believe." The voice asserted with full emphasis: "Indeed it is true. She has already completed the ceremony to our full satisfaction. You may ask the Sun-god, the progenitor of our dynasty."

When Rama invoked the Sun-god to get confirmation, the deity said that Sita had done that very religiously and that there was no need to repeat the ceremony. Rama and Lakshmana were ashamed that they doubted Sita's word. They were now very much impressed with the power of her virtue. But Sita was unhappy with the witnesses she had produced and which refused to confirm all that she had done. Then she cursed the Phalgu river that henceforth it would be flowing only underground. She cursed the Ketaki flower that henceforth it would not be accepted by Lord Shiv in his worship. She cursed the cow that henceforth her mouth would be considered impure. But the remaining section of the cow would remain, however, pure as ever. And finally she cursed the fire that it would have to consume everything indiscriminately. "That is the reason why Ketaki flower is not allowed in Shiv's worship," concluded Romaharshan.

❑❑

13.
Shiv Prohibits Champaka Flower In His Worship

After a pause he started to tell that why a champak flower became unacceptable to Lord Shiva.

In the holy teertha of Gokarna there was a temple dedicated to Lord Shiva. Narada once decided to visit this temple. On way he spiked a beautiful flowering Champaka tree and stopped to admire it. At that time a brahmana happened to reach there to pluck flowers from the tree. But seeing Narada there he refrained from plucking the flowers.

Then Narada, out of curiosity, asked: "What are you doing here? Where are you going?" While hiding his real intention and lying, the brahmana said: "I am going to beg alms."

Narada went to the temple. Meanwhile the brahamana plucked the flowers from the Champaka tree and placed them in a basket that he covered up well. Narada once again met the brahmana and accosted him: "Where are you going now?

The brahamana again lied. "Back home," adding "I coundn't get any alms.

Now Narada was suspicious. He went to the Champaka tree and asked : "Has that brahman plucked any flowers?"

"What brahamana?" replied the tree. "I don't know any brahamana. No one has plucked any flowers.

Still sensing suspicion, Narada went back to the temple. There he discovered fresh Champaka flowers lying there on the top of the Shiv Linga.There was another devotee praying silently. Narada asked him.: "Did you see any one coming to worship the 'linga' with the fresh Champaka flowers?"

"Yes I did," replied the devotee "It was an evil brahmana. He worships Shiv everyday with the Champaka flowers. Thanks to Shiv's blessings, he has managed to completely brain wash the king of the area and has recently been steeling the king's wealth. Despite being a brahamana he makes the king cause harm to other brahmanas to serve his evil ends."

The divine sage, Narada, then asked Lord Shiv : "Why do you encourage such evil ?"

"I am helpless," Shiv said : "I cannot resist if anyone worships me with the Champaka flowers."

It was exactly that moment a brahmana woman came running with her tale of woe. Her husband was crippled. Nevertheless she could receive some money from the king so that she could perform the marriage of her nubile daughter. The king was kind enough to give her a cow as well in alms. But now that evil brahmana was insisting to get half of the gifts from the king since it was due to his good offices that the king had been so generous. "That evil brahmana has already snatched half of the money, "She said, adding, "But how a cow is to be divided?"

Hearing her tale of woe Narada then decided that something ought to be done about the Champaka tree and that evil brahmana. Apart from everythintg else, the champaka tree was a liar. Narada cursed the Champaka tree that henceforth its flowers would never be accepted by Shiv as an offering. He then cursed that evil brahmana that in next life he would be born as a 'rakshasa' (demon) named Viradha. But since the brahmana was also a devotee of Shiv the curse was modified that Viradha would meet his death at Rama's hands and would then be born again as a brahmana.

□□

14.

The Tales Related To Ganesh

Lord Shiv and Parvati-the eternal spouses had a son known as Ganesh or Ganapati. The very name makes him the head of a group, for 'Gana' means a group. How he was born and how he acquired this name have many legends interwoven with the actual story. Briefly they are given below.

(i) Birth of Ganesh

Once Goddess Parvati was roaming around with her two female companions called Jaya and Vijaya. Then, during the course of their talk they lodged a complaint with Parvati. "O Mahadevi (Great Goddess) ! All the gatekeepers owe their allegiance exclusively to Lord Shankar and we, the female-folk, have no control over them. At times, we need absolute privacy but they allow all to come into our apartments even at the most awkward moments. Pardon our saying this but the most untimely intruder is none other than your spouse, Lord Shankar. Since he doesn't have his time marked as he himself is the Lord of Mahakaal (or The Ruler of Time), he has a habit of intruding into the ladies' section at most awkward moment." Parvati shot back, enraged at her dear Lord being termed as an intruder. "Hold your tongue, Jaya and Vijaya ! Do you know what you are babbling? Lord is my husband and how could he be checked from entering into his espouse's apartment ? If you both feel inconvenienced, I will make arrangements for your separate stay."

"No, Mahadevi," both pleaded, "what we are saying is not for our inconvenience but yours as well. There are occasions when a lady needs total privacy, even from her husband. Like the time you are taking bath or cleaning your body. That it a very awkward moment for anybody to come in, be him Lord Shankar himself. Don't you feel so ?"

Parvati replied thoughtfully: "Yes,-I feel you are right, That day when I was having my bath I was rather inconvenienced by Lord's sudden intrusion. Now I understand what you say. We must have our own gatekeeper to watch our section."

Jaya and Vijaya were happy that the Mahadevi realised the urgency and importance of what they were driving at. "But how to get such a watchman who should owe his allegiance only to yourself," Jaya raised the query.

"Yes," supported Vijaya : "Here all the ganas (henchmen) owe their allegiance only to Lord Shankar."

"Don't worry," reassured Goddess Parvati and there and then she created a boy by her own filth and scurf. Giving him a staff to guard the gate, Parvati went in to relax.

That time, Lord Shankar was out of Kailash. When he returned after some days, he rushed in straight to Parvati's chamber. But there he found a teenaged boy with a staff in his hand obstructing Lord's access to Parvati's chamber. The boy was extremely good looking and powerful. Shiv was taken back when stopped from entering. "Do you know who am I ? I am Shankar, the spouse of Parvati ! I am her husband and owner of this place. I have free access to entire Universe, let alone my wife's chamber. But who are you to stop me. I never saw you before." "Never mind who I am," replied the defiant boy.

"My mother is taking her bath and I just cannot allow you to enter. You should come later."

Now, Lord Shankar was enraged.

"Hey you fool of a boy ! You call Parvati your mother ! It means I am your father ! Why should you stop me ?"

"Whatever you be," the boy replied sternly , "I can't allow you to go in till my mother says so. She is taking her bath and she had given specific instructions not to allow anyone in. I am sorry !"

Now Lord Shiv was furious. How could this unknown boy challenge his authority in his own house? He summoned his 'Ganas' and asked them to tell this boy who he was and what authority he exercised in the entire Kailash (the dwelling place of Lord shiv).

The 'ganas' went near the boy and tried their best to impress upon the boy to allow the Lord to go in. But their entire effort produced no change in the boy's stand. "It is not good for you also to invite Lord's wrath," they pleaded. But the boy refused to budge, saying : "I don't care for myself, but I must obey my mother's instructions. Whoever he be, he cannot go in till my mother has taken her bath."

At last, the henchmen of Lord Shiv began to fight with the boy who proved to be no novice in retaliation. He cast such severe blows by his staff that the 'ganas' of Lord Shiv had to beat a hasty retreat, vanquished and wounded.

At that time the cosmic sage, Narada, happened to be visiting Kailash. For Narada, even otherwise,no place is believed to be inaccessible in the universe. When he saw the commotion, he rushed back to the divine realm to apprise Indra and other celestials of the queer happening at Kailash. Brahma, the Creator, was also told. Deeming himself to be the seniormost of the celestials, Brahma first went to explain things to that delinquent boy. But let alone his listening to the celestial grandpa, the boy merrily plucked at the flowing beard of Brahma, causing him pain and injury. Though the Creator introduced himself aloud, the boy didn't care for that., When Brahma still persisted, the boy lifted a nailed staff left by the Shiv's henchmen, and hurled it at Brahma, who returned, grieving and injured, to apprise Shiv of his sorry tale.

Hearing about that indomitable boy, Lord Shiv and Lord Vishnu left with a huge army of the celestials to teach that urchin a lesson. But undaunted by that huge force, the boy began to fight with redoubled vigour. First of all Lord Vishnu came to the forefront who was greeted by the boy with a deadly missile. Lord Vishnu was taken aback. He had won so many ferocious demons but that boy, proved to be a mightier opponent. Seeing lord Vishnu retreat, Lord Shiv himself came ahead and launched a renewed attack. But that boy far from getting subdued, cast a pointed mace to make Lord Shiv lose his famous bow, Pinaak.

Now Lord Shiv blew up in anger. "Enough of it, you silly urchin," and saying so he hurled his renowned trident to hack off that boy's head !

That mischievous and mysterious boy had almost pulverised all the gods by his valour. Many of them felt that boy was a plant of the demons who by their black power had made that boy almost invincible. When the boy's trunk fell, it made a horrible sound. So powerful it was that Parvati, who, all this while was merrily bathing, rushed out only to see his son beheaded. At once she, having know all that had transpired, created about a hundred thousand deadly powers and commanded them to devour all the celestial. So angry was she that even her spouse, Lord Shankar, could hardly summon enough courage to face her. Hearing her severe command, all the celestials thought that their end was high. They felt so powerless and emaciated before those deadly powers that their total destruction appeared to be a foregone conclusion. At that crucial moment, Narad came forward and began to sing orisons to placate Parvati who then appeared to be a live personification of wrath. It was after a long period that she could again be somewhat calm. Then she was told by Narada that her son was killed in a confusion. "O Goddess," Narad pleaded: "Your son had been the mightiest existence in the world. Such a brave and chivalrous boy has never been seen either among the demons or the gods. We all are very sorry at his death. What should we do to receive your benign affection again !"

"You can get that only on one condition," replied the Goddess with a stern face: "Revive my son back to life and declare him to be the foremost god among all the celestials."

The condition was readily accepted. But how to revive a headless-body ? Then Lord Shankar, who had by this time known that it was he who had beheaded his own son, sent messangers to find someone or some creature who had been born on the same day and at the same time. That creature's head was to be planted on that boy's trunk. Since by Mother Parvati's condition that boy was declared to be the head of the group, he came to be known as 'Ganesh'. The only creature to be found was an elephant, so cutting off its head, the messangers brought it and it was placed on Ganesha's shoulders to make him once again a living being.

Another legend of Lord Ganesh's birth gives a different story. It says that one night when Parvati was sleeping on her soft and embroidered milk-white couch in her palace in Kailash Lord Vishnu appeared, clad as a priest, apparently old and weak from starvation. Then he begged for food. Lord Shiv and Parvati greeted him kindly and asked him what he desired. He told them that he would like to become their son, and immediately that preist, took the form of a tiny baby. That child quickly lay on Parvati's bed, staring at the ceiling and waving his hand and feet merrily, like the new-born children do. So perfect was that boy's physique that it was sheer delight to look at him.

Getting Vishnu as their tiny son, Lord Shiva and Parvati were delighted, Getting the message all the gods and goddesses circled that baby to give their blessing. Vishnu gave him the blessing of knowledge, Brahma of fame and worship, Lord Dharma of righteousness and mercy, Lord Shiv of generosity, intelligence, peace and self control. Goddess Lakshmi promised to ever dwell at the place where Lord Ganesh is adored. Goddess Saraswati gave him power of speech, memory and eloquence, Savitri gave him all wisdom.

All those who were present there included Saturn, which is an accursed deity or planet. As all those versed in astrology know that Saturn's aspect is believed to be deadly. So, Saturn knew that if he looked towards that son of Parvati's that child was sure to be troubled. But like all those present there, he also wanted to look at that beautiful child. He asked if he could see the child and approached Parvati who was seated on her throne of precious stones, holding the child on her lap. But he advanced with his head bent, and Parvati, after greeting him, asked why he did not looked at her or the child? There upon Saturn humbly submitted : "O Goddess ! Everyone has to bear the fruit of their actions, even I myself. One day I was sitting so engrossed in my worship that I did not look at my beautiful wife who had approached in an amorous mood. She felt slighted and therefore cursed him that henceforth whatever I looked at would be destroyed. So I dared neither to look at the child or at you !" Hearing this, Goddess Parvati laughed, and told him he must look at the child and her.

But Saturn knew how dreadful his sight (or aspect) was. So he could not decide whether to look or not for either way it would lead to bad result. After much deliberation he decided to glance out of the corner of his eye at the child only. But even a glance was sufficient, and immediately the child's head vanished. Parvati wept bitterly and then fainted at the disaster, which had stunned all other gods and goddesses to silence. What an inauspicious happening in the house celebrating an auspicious event !

Then Vishnu, whose incarnation that child was, flew away on Garud, his favourite bird-vehicle, to a forest in the north where, on the bank of a river, he saw a king elephant asleep. He hacked off the pachyderm's head with his Chakra (discus) and returned to Kailash, and placed the head of the elephant on the headless child. Hence Ganesh has an elephant head.

Another legend gives other details of Lord Ganesh's birth. It says that once Narad asked Vishnu that since all beings get what is their due, why Ganesh got an elephant's head when the world is full of beautiful things. Why didn't he bring a human head for Ganesh ? Then Lord Vishnu explained : "O Sage ! This was Ganesh's destiny. Once the lord of sages, 'Durvasa' (a sage known for his very short temper) had been given a flower from the holy Paarijaata tree which came from the Churning of the Ocean of Milk, and he gave it to Indra. This flower was capable of destroying all obstacles and it was so sacrosanct that he who wore it on his head was to be the ruler of all the world. The Goddess of Fortune, Lakshmi was to ever remain with the person keeping the flower. His powers were to be greater than all the powers that all the celestials comand. But Indra, absent-mindedly threw that flower on to the head of his favourite elephant Airavat, who went to the forest and tossed it away. This was the elephant whose head was placed on Ganesh's shoulders!"

Another story tells the reason why Lord Shiv was destined to have such a son. This Purana records that once Shiv, in trying to kill some demons, struck the sun with his trident and caused that great god to fall from his chariot and lose consciousness. All the gods panicked at the fall of this god of light and glory. When the sage Kashyap, father of the sun, heard about his dear son's fall, he cursed Shiv, saying that the head of his son would be cut off. Although Lord Shiv had revived the sun, the curse remained, which showed its effect in Ganesh's losing his head.

According to another legend, Lord Ganesh was conjured out of a piece of cloth by Lord Shiv to make a son for Parvati. It is said that even after a thousand years when Shiv and Parvati did not get a son, the latter, like a normal woman, was extremely sad on this account. Lord Shiv loved his wife immensely and he could not tolerate his espouse's this grief. So, he decided to conjure up a son out of a piece of cloth. Later, Shiv himself brought about the boy's death by decapitation and then, in order to placate Parvati, he called the gods to find a new head. After much searching they gave him an elephant head which had a tusk broken when it was cut from the body.

Normally Ganesh's head is always shown as having only one tusk but some apocryphal account refer him to be having the normal two tusked head. One of the tusk was broken in Ganesh's fight with Parashurama. It is said that once Parashuram-another incarnation of Lord Vishnu and famous for his quick temper and the axe-came to visit Ganesh's father Lord Shiv. As Shiv was asleep Ganesh would not let Parashuram pass, and they fought. In that fight Ganesh managed to wrap his trunk round the body of Parashuram and swinging him round and round, threw him away. Parshuram was thrown with such a force that he lost his consciousness the moment he fell on the ground. When Parashuram recovered his consciousness, he threw his axe at Ganesh. This axe was famous, for it had been given to Parashuram by Lord Shiv himself, and recognising it, Ganesh could not fight against it But he let it fall on his one tusk, cutting it off.

This way there are many legends woven into the birth-story of Lord Ganesh. Out of these the most popular and commonly accepted legend is the First one which has been given in detail.

(ii) Marriage of Lord Ganesh

Lord Ganesh is the youngest child of Parvati and Shiv and most favourite of his mother. Ganesh's elder brother is Karitkeya or Skand or Subramaniyam. Both the boys had grown together and were devoted companions, though Kartikeya had come from Lord Shiv's seed, and represented his destructive aspect, while Ganesh had come from Parvati. so he represented the constructive aspect of the Mother Goddess.

When both turned nubile, their parents began to search brides for their marriage. Lord Shiv and Parvati discussed between themselves which of their sons should be married first. As they could not decide they called the boys together and told them that, as they loved them both equally, they could not decide who should be married first. They suggested, however, that one who would encircle the earth first, should be married first.

Now, Kartikeya had the martian qualities—as he represents Mars, the god of war. He had his vehicle peacock. While Ganesh was more interested in sedentary works, perhaps because of his size and also as he has a mouse for vehicle. Hearing about their parent's decision that he who encircled the earth first would be married first, Kartikeya started out immedialely, and began his travel round the world. Ganesh remained at home wondering what he could do, for, because of his size and his tiny vehicle, he knew that he couldn't have defeated his brother in the race. So, where physique created an impediment, he used his mind to win his point. Pondering over the problem he hit upon a brilliant solution. He took the ceremonial bath and asked his parents to sit on their thrones while he worshipped them. He went round them seven times, and sang their praises. Then he requested his parents to arrange his marriage.

But Lord Shiv and Parvati reminded him that he must first go round the earth and advised him to go quickly so that he could come back the more quickly. But brilliaint Ganesh answered : "O Sire! I have encircled the earth. The scriptures say that parents who bring the son to the world are verily the entire world themselves for the son. It is said that to encircle the parents is equal to a pilgrimage round the earth. But, on the other hand, if anyone leaves his parents unattended in order to encircle the earth or go on pilgrimage, he is guilty of a crime. Hence you must arrange for my marriage and prepare to punish the elder brother when he returns home."

Lord Shiv and Goddess Parvati found this argument uncuttable. They saw the truth in what their brilliant son had said and arranged for his marriage to the two daughters of Praja-pati. [Prajapati literally means the protector of people. It is a mythological existence created to care for the Praja or people. Praja-pati is also called the Lord of Creatures.] He had two daughters named 'Riddhi' (prosperity or affluence) and 'Siddhi' (attainment, or adeptness). Both the daughters were married to Ganesh. All the gods came to the ceremony which

---

1. **Some mythological accounts give the name of Ganesh's wife as 'Buddhi'**
   (wisdom) and Siddhi.

47

was performed by Vishwa-karma (the Architect of the world). In due time two sons were born. Siddh's son was called Kshema (welfare) and Riddhi's called Laabh (gain).

Everyone was happy until one day the elder son Kartikeya returned after encircling the earth. As he came near his home, he met Narada. He told Kartikeya all that had transpired in the latter's absence and advised him to leave again, for no wise man who wanted peace and justice would look "upon the face of those who gravely wrong him." Kartikeya took the advice and, after telling his parents that they had wronged him greatly, left and went to the mountain in deep south called the Mountain of Krauncha (the Heron). He felt bitterly cheated by his parents.

When Parvati heard about her elder son's self imposed exile, she was very sad. Although Ganesh had been their favourite son, she was also mother of Kartikeya. When she could not be placated, to satisfy her, Shiv sent a part of himself to dwell in that mountain and they both visited their son. But Kartikey a was still angry and moved away, even though all the gods begged him to remain there. Ever since then, Lord Shiv visits him on the day of the new moon and Parvaii on the day of the full moon.

(iii) Ganesh as the Lord of Scribes

Ganesh is described to be a great scribe who had mastered all the religious lore and scriptures. It was he who was invoked by the great sage Vedvyas to write "Mahabharat", as dictated by the sage. The related legend is as follows:

The Great Sage Vedvyas was worried about the continued existence of the holy Vedas owing to the surfacing of the demonical tendencies on the earth. People had started interpreting the Vedas according to their convenience. To safeguard the Vedas and maintain their sanctity, sage Vedvyas thought of bringing all the knowledge under one compendium. With this intention he began to mentally create "Mahabharat"—with the base story of the struggle between the Kauravas and the Pandavas—having many interwoven tales which carried the essence of all the ancient learning. Vedvyas kept on mentally composing his shlokas and when the process was complele, he desired to bring his composition in a book form—very well written. Now to pen down a compendium containing more than a lakh shlokas

48

created another problem. The sage wanted an expert scribe who could write this, dictated by him.

When he could not get a desired scribe, he worshipped the Creator, Brahma. When the Creator put in an appearence before him, the sage requested: "O Lord, I have mentally created a compendium of all our knowledge. Nothing that is not in it, is useful to mankind and what-ever is not in it is not available anywhere else. Now I want a good writer who could write it for me. 1 will dictate the entire compendium. I request you to get me such a competent scribe."

"My son." replied the Creator. "I am glad you decided to put all our knowledge in one 'Grantha'. Only Lord Ganesh is competent to accomplish this job. You must pray him to do so for you."

Getting this advice, the sage sat on his seat and began to invoke Lord Ganesh. In a trice he appeared before him. When Vedvyas explained the Lord his problem, the latter said: "Do not worry, O great sage ? I will do it for you. But on one condition! Once I start writing, my pen should not stop even for a moment Only if you can dictate it non-stop then I can take up this assignment for your convenience." Vedvyas was somewhat unnerved by this condition. Although the whole 'Granth' was in his memory, he intended it to edit it while dictating it. In that case he could not have dictated it non stop. But pondering over the issue, he hit upon a solution, and he requested the Lord: "All-right. Lord. I accept your condition. But you will have to accede to one more request of mine. You shall not write anything without understanding the meaning of the Shlokas dictated by me."

"All right !" replied the Lord, "I will not write anything without understanding its proper meaning."

And then the sage Vedvyas began to dictate his "Mahabharat" and Lord Ganesh began to write it. To get more time for creating new Shlokas the sage used to dictate some of very terse shlokas known as Koot-Shloka[2]. In these the real meaning could not be derived

---

2. Koot literally means a hill or a heap. Later it came to be used as a shield to hide the real meaning. Hence 'Koot' means something hidden under the heap. Something that is not apparent or clear or which can have multiple meaning or intepretations. Here Koot meeans those terse compositions ofthe sage whose meaning is not easily decipherable as they are in a sort of the puzzle form.

easily.Convoluted as they were by various kuns and word-plays, even Lord Ganesh took sometime to understand their real meaning, during which the sage used to create very many other shlokas so that his flow of dictation never stopped. When it was written completely Lord Ganesh left after blessing Vedvyas: "Sage, your's this grantha shall never be destroyed and its importance shall glow with time."

Indeed, it is the most time-tested treatise on ancient learning which appears ever relevant and important.

(iv) Ganehs's Role in the Destruction of Tripur

The Shiva-Purana records that Skanda s creation was caused by the celestials to have the deadly demon named Tarak slayed. After the demon was slayed, his three sons Tarakaksha,Vidyunmali and Kamalaksha felt shelterless and in order to gain supreme strength, the three some began to perform a rigorous penance to propitiate Lord Brahma, who eventually appeared before them:

"Ask your boon! "theCreator said.

Then they asked for the boon by virtue of which they might not be killed by anyone save Lord Shiv, and requested the Creator to grant them three well-made cities as they had been rendered shelterless by their father's death. Then Brahma asked Maya Danav, the architect of the demons to create three beautiful cities each for one son of Tarakasur. "Then he wrought one city of gold for Tarakaksha, of silver for Vidyunmali and of iron for Kamalaksha. But soon they became very powerful as much as to trouble the celestials. Although they had propitiated Lord Shiv--their Nemesis, Lord Vishnu for the benefit of the gods created as much confusion as to make Lord Shiv eventually get ready to slay the three demons and destroy their three cities combinedly known as Tripur. But the moment Lord Shiv set his deadly arrow upon his sturdy and renowned bow and took the aim, Ganesh was standing close and he created an obstacle in between to the great chagrin of his father and the celestials. Lord Shiv was furious- When the gods asked why did he do so, Ganesha replied: "Although all of you have given word to my mother, none of you is keeping it. Not even my father is careful about it. You all promised to my mother, it is always I who is to be worshipped first. But I found none of you caring for your word. I created this obstacle to remind you all of your promise to my mother."

The gods realised their mistake and worshipped lord Ganesh there and then. Since then, it is a standard practice to worship Lord Ganesh first not as much out of devotion to him but out of fear of his illimitable capacity to create hurdle. Hence his one of the epithet is Vighneshwar or master of all obstacles.

(V) Name of Lord Ganesh

Lord Ganesh is the most favoured Lord of the Hindu Pantheon and no worship is deemed to be of any value unless he is worshipped initially. It is due to the effect of the boon that his mother Parvati had received from all the gods, as already mentioned.

The god has twelve names which have been mentioned with an explanatory note for their meanings.

1. *Ganapati* or *Ganaadhipati* or *Ganesh* : All the three mean lord or master of a group. Gana literally means 'a flock, multitude, group, troop, collection.' In this context it means a body of followers or attendants or demi gods who were Lord Shiv's henchmen. Ganesh means head of such a group. Also, since he is always to be adored First among all gods for worship, he can be considered to be the head of all the gods. However, the general meaning derived from this word 'Ganesh' would be "the Lord of the numbered;" that is, the Lord of all things, for whom we speak of things-the differentiated aspects of one—we are dealing with that which can be numbered or counted.

2. *Umaputra* : Meaning the son of Uma or Parvati.

3. *Heramba* : An epithet for Ganesh, it also mean 'mother's pet.'

4. *Vinayak* : It also means an especial leader or the leader with especial qualities.

5. *Gajaanana* : Meaning elephant-faced or having face of an elephant.

6. *Sarva-Siddhanta* : Meaning capable of making everything possible or he who is capable of providing every Siddhi (adeptness) to his worshipper.

7. *Ekadanta* : Meaning one tusked.This epithet of Ganesh belies the legend saying that he was originally a two tusked

51

elephant face and his one tusk was broken in his fight with Parshuram. Even in the oldest works this epithet appears.

8. *Lambodara* : Meaning one with a long or huge belly.
9. *Musikvaahan* : Meaning he who has the mouse as his favourite vehicle.
10. *Vakratunda* : One who has askew proboscis.
11. *Vighneshwar* : The lord of all obstacles (for detailed explanation see ahead)
12. *Krishnapingaaksha* : It means one who has black and yellowish brown eyes.

Allthough there are more names, these are the popular once. In fact all these names signify the salient features of the body of a god. Other less known names are Kapil, Gajakarna, Vikat, Dhomravarna and Bhaalchandra, the last name being common for both father and son, that is, Lord Shiv and Ganesh, for both are described lo be having the moon reposing upon their foreheads.

Although the fourth Day of the bright half of every lunar month is believed to be the day of Lord Ganesh, the Magh (15 th Jan. to 15 th Feb), Bhadrapad (Aug. - Sept.) and the full moon day of Vaishakh are held to be the special days for Lord Ganesh's worship.

❑❑

15.

The Tales Related to Kartikeya

Why Kartikeya's birth had become a necessity for the gods has already been given in details in the previous pages. Here only missing events shall be described.

Following Shiv's marriage with Parvati, the newly wed couple stayed for some time at Himavant's place. Then Shiv and Uma (Parvati) left for Kailash visiting many mountain peaks on the way. Time continued to pass merrily.

Meanwhile the gods became panicky seeing the almost unending "Honey Moon' of the Eternal Couple. The gods requested Shiv to stop his love-play and fulfil their need by producing a son. Shiv eventually agreed but asked them as to what was to be done with the seed that had been discharged. Lord Agni, representing the god's case readily agreed to accept that seed, getting into the form of a pigeon. But it was so powerful that Agni failed to carry it. Then Shiv advised him to have it planted in the womb of some woman. Then as advised by Brahma, Agni took bath in the holy teertha of Prayag (the holy confluence of the sacred rivers) and there it was planted in the wombs of the the six wives' of the Holy Sages through their pores of the skin via the Ganga which had been its intermediate repository.But unable to bear the heat of the seed she had it transplaned into the wombs of the Krithikas (the Holy Sages' wives). All those six wives became pregnant and their husbands deserted them on the charge of adultery. They all began to dwell at the Himalayas. At due

---

1. Pleiades, astronomically a group of six naked-eyed and a multititude of telescopic stars in the shouder of the sign TAURUS.

time they all delivered and each of them threw the foetus back into the Ganga river. Even the Ganga couldn't bear their combined form and threw it on the forest of reeds. There on the sixth day of the bright half of the lunar month Margshirsha came into existence, this son of Lord Shiv. Since he was the product of six wombs he had six faces. Hence his one of the names was Shadanan or the six-faced. He is known by many names, prominent among which are Kartikeya, Skanda, Murugan and Subramanyam. Soon the news spread all over the world to the greatest delight of the gods. All this while Shiv was unaware of these tidings. Once Uma asked him about his seed he had given to Agni. "Has it been wasted?" she asked. Then Shiv inquired and learnt about the birth of Kartikeya. They immediately repaired to the mount the child was dwelling on, fostered by the divine female existance called Krithikas. Since they were his foster mother he earned the epithet Kartikeya which means "of the Krithikas." Soon Uma and Shiv reached there and were delighted to meet their son. Then they escorted their son lovingly, back to Kailash. Uma was sorry to have been deprived of the happiness of becoming a mother-producing the child from her own womb. When she learnt about the gods' scheme to get the seed of Shiv, she cursed all divine ladies that they shall ever remain uncapable of producing any child.

Kartikeya in due time grew to be a young lad. Indra and other gods approached Shiv asking if the youth could now fight Tarakasur. Shiv agreed and appointed Kartikeva. the commander of the divine forces, and Kartikeya went with the gods to Indra's heavenly city. He was presented with the choicest divine weapons by various gods while going to Indra's capital Amravati where he saw the damage wrought by Tarak and became very angry, itching now for the fray. Preparation for the battle began. The gods rode on their vehicles, Kartikeya on a peacock, which he chose as his favourite mount. Indra came on his elephant Airavat, Agni on a ram, Yama on a buffalo and Varuna on a dolphin. This strange array struck terror into Taraka's forces and his soldiers wanted to retire at once. But Taraka, brandishing his sword and laughing with contempt, rushed into the battle. The fight lasted for long with no real victory on either side until Taraka tried to destroy the gods with his magic arms. Then Kartikeya went to their rescue and a duel began between the two leaders. Taraka used all his magic weapons he had from the god of fire and the god of wind but Kartikeya neutralised these and finally plunged his lance into demon and killed him.

Having killed Taraka and fulfilled the mission he was born for Kartikeya was immediately hailed as the nayaka or the commander-in-chief of the divine forces for ever. It is mentioned in this Puranas that after Kartikeva slayed Taraka, his fame spread far and wide, making many kings and gods come to him for having their enemies slain. There was once a king from the Kroncha (Heron) mount who was constantly troubled by Banasur. He came to request Kartikeya to kill that demon which the divine commander did easily. Kartikeya is also represented by Mars or the god of war. His mount is a peacock and the seat is the Krauncha mount. When he went to kill Banasur he liked the mount so much and almost settled their after his tiff with his parents. He became unhappy with his parents when he found them to be showing partiality to his younger brother, Ganesh.

When Lord Shiv and Parvati saw their two sons coming of age, they discussed as to whose marriage should be solemnised first. Although Kartikeya was elder one, owing to his physique Ganesh looked senior between the two. Both the boys had grown up together and were devoted companions, though Kartikeya represented more of Shiv's distructive aspect, being born of Shiv's seed, while Ganesh, born of Parvati's body's scurf represented the Eternal Pair's constructive aspect. When Shiv and Parvati could not decide who between their sons should be married first, they called the boys together and told them that, as they loved them equally, they couldn't decide this problem. They suggested, however, that they had devised a noble plan to settle the matter. He who would make the full round of the earth first would also be the first to get married.

Although Ganesh, like his brother agreed to the condition, this competition was not to his liking. Because of his heavy size and the mouse as his mount he was not likely to win the contest against Kartikeya who had a fine body and the peacock as his mount. While Kartikeya started out immedialtely and began his travel round the world, Ganesha remained at home wondering what to do. At last the solution occurred to him. He took the ceremonial bath and asked his parents to sit on their thrones while he worshipped them. On being reminded about the contest by his parents Ganesh shrewdly answered that he had encircled the earth. On being asked how, he replied taking recourse of the scriptural assertion that parents formed the entire creation for the progeny. His going round the parents was tentamount to his encircling the entire earth. His parents found his argument quite convincing and arranged for his marriage to the two daughters of the Praja-pati Riddhi and Siddhi. All the gods came to the ceremony which was performed by Vishwakarma the divine architect.

Meanwhile, Kartikeya was on his world tour. When he learnt about Ganesh's marriage, he was sore and in a sulking mood retired to the Kraunch Mount deep south. When Parvati and Mahadeva learnt about the anger of their eldest son they were very much sorry. Then Paravati, in order to humour her estranged son decided to send a part of herself to dwell in that mount. Then, after the ceremony was over, both of them visited Kartikeya. But he was still angry and moved away. And the Purana say, that ever since then, Shiv visits him on the day of the new moon day and Parvati on the full moon day.

Kartikeya is also known as Skanda. While he was a boy, Indra unknowingly fought with him and was defeated. It is said when Indra buried his thunderbold on the left and right and center of Kartikeya's body, three persons emerged from the three wounds : "Shaakh", "Vishaakla" and "Nigam". Aided by these three when Kartikeya again challenged Indra he ran away and later apologised. Since then these four persons verily one person's parts - came to be combined by known as Skanda. Thus Kartikeya helped the gods and became their god to war.

Kartikeya has many names. In fact most of his epithets have reference to the circumstances relating to his birth. Since Shiv had first cast his seed into Agni, he is called Agnibhoo. When Agni, unable to bear that hot seed threw it into Ganga, Kartikeya came to be known as Gangaputra. Then the seed was transferred to six Krittikkas- when they went to take their bath in the Ganges. Hence his name is Kartikeya. Since he had six faces he is known as Shadanan or Shadrupa.

According to yet another account of his birth, the seed of Shiv was cast by the ganges into a thicket of the reed called Saravana. Hence his name is Saravanabhoo or Sarajanman. Since his abode is at the Kraunch mount his name became 'Kraunchadarana'. He is Nayak because he commanded the divine army. His defeating Taraka won him another epithet : Tarakajit.

He is often called Mars or Mangal because he was the commander-in-chief of the divine forces-a position attributed to Mars or Mangal. In South India he is worshipped also by two additional names: Subramanya and Murugan.

Kartikaya rides on his peacock and he is described to be having one wife: Devasena or Valli. In his hands he holds a Shakti (kind of spear), arrow, sword, discus, noose, cock, bow, shield, conch, plough with one hand in the gesture of giving a boon ('Vardan') and the other in assuring his devotees i.e., Abhaya Mudra. He is thus regarded as the god of war and as in many shaivite temples, a guardian deity.

❏❏

16.

The Tales Relating To Jyotirlinga Teerthas

A linga is an image of Shiv. This though literally means a phallus, in the context of Shiv it represents all that Shiv stands for. There are several lingas. the Shiv-Purana claims that whichever place where the Shiv devotees congregate, there Shiv manifests himself in the form of a linga.

Among all the lingas there are twelve 'Jyotirlinga' i.e. especially consecrated symbols of Shiv which are spread almost throughout the Aryavarta (ancient name of undivided India). The places where these 'Jyotirlingas' are they become especially hallowed. These twelve Jyotirlingas are Somanath, Mallikarjuna, Mahakala, Omkara, Kedara, Bhimshankara, Vishwanatha, Trymbaka, Vaidyanatha, Nagesha, Rameshwara and Ghushnesha. The tales relating to their aquiring the followed states are given below.

(i) Somnatha and The Moon god

As mentioned before Daksha had 60 daughters out of which 27 were married to the moon-god, Chandra. But Chandra loved Rohini, one of his 27 wifes most, to the great chagrin of his other wives who felt quite neglected by their common husband Chandra. The remaining 26 wives went to their father,Daksha and complained about their husband's partial behaviour. Allthough Daksha repeatedly warned his son-in-law to devote his equal attention to all his wives, Chandra didn't heard to his warning. When Chandra continued to neglect all others except Rohini among his wife, Daksha was enraged and cursed the moon (Chandra) that he would gradually fade away. When

Chandara found-that the curse started showing his affect and his shine started fading, he was nervous. At once he sought Brahma's advice but Brahma told him that only Shiva could solve his problem. Chandra straight away rushed to Prabhasa Teertha (on the west coast in modern Gujarat). He built a beautiful linga on the bank of the river Saraswati which flew near the ocean, and started worshipping Lord Shiva. He continued to pray Shiv for six months at a stretch.

At the end of that Tapasya, Shiv, pleased with the moon god's worship appeared before him.

"Ask you boon, O Chandra !' said the Lord of the universe.

Chandra then apprised him of the severe problem he had been facing due to Daksha's curse. Giving a thought to the problem, Lord Shiv said : "Well ! Daksha's curse cannot be entirely ignored. This much modification I can suggest that during the dark half you will wane in accordance with the effect of the curse. But I allow you to wax again in the Shuklapaksha (the bright half) to regain your best glory in entirety. I will see to it that Daksha accepts this arrangement. This, I hope, would satisfy every body."

Chandra was immensely relieved with this modification in the curse. At least he had a chance of aquiring his best glory. The linga to which Chandra prayed is the Joytirlinga of Somanatha. The Purana says that Shiv remains ever present in Somanatha, a famous teertha now on the coast of Gujarat.

(ii) Mallikarjuna[1]

As has already been recounted that Kartikeya felt Cheated when Shiv and Parvati allowed Ganesh to marry first. He felt so angry that he decided not to live with Shiv and Parvati any longer. Under protest he left kailash for good and had began to dwell at the mountain Kraunch.

His decision had quite pained his parents. Particularly Parvati felt quite miserable at her son's leaving her for good. Not understanding her son's this decision she still kept on sending gods sages, Gandharavas and Apsaras to bring her son back to her. But adamant as he was, Kartikeya refused to come back. Even when Shiva

---

1. Here Shiv is called Arjuna and Paravati Mallika, hence the name.

and Parvati themselves went to visit kartikeya, Kartikeya kept on evading them and never coming too close to her parents.

At last Shiv and Parvati started to live at a place that was about six miles away from where their estranged son was living, so as to keep the possibility open for wooing Kartikeya. The place they lived came to be known as Mallikarjuna which, later on, devoloped into a hallowed place for the devotees of Shiva in Tamilnadu in modern times.

(iii) Dooshana and Mahakala[1]

This temple of Mahakala houses the third Joytirlinga. It is situated in the city of Ujjain which in ancient time was called Ujjaini Its another name was Avanti. It is situated on the bank of the river Kshipra.

Eons ago there lived a brahmana in the citi of Avanti. His name was Vedpriya. He was a staunch devotee of Lord Shiv and he had devoloped his four sons also in the same tradition. He would devotedly worship Shiva everyday, accompanied by his four sons named Devapriya, Priyamadha, Suvrita and Suvrata.

Not far away from the city, there lived a demon (Asura) on a hill named Ratanmala. His name was Dooshana. Although the demon was not as much evil- minded as the 'Asuras' used to be, he was averse to following the dictates of the Vedas and following faith prescribed by the Vedic text. So he went about destroying the adherents of such a prescribed religion wherever he could. In the process of his sojourns to the city for this purpose he also learnt that there lived four brahmanas in Avanti who worshipped Lord Shiva very devoutly, By the time he could learn about the four sons, their father Vedapriya had expired.

One day he attacked the city with his cohorts. They threatened to kill the four brahmans but the devout brothers were not unnerved. Undaunted they continued the worship of Shiva and kept on religiously bowing before the Linga everyday.

---

1. This is a symbolic term. It is believed that in ancient India this temple was the observatory for reckoning time like the greenwich observatory is now for the entire world. Since shiv is the controller of time, he is also called Mahakala.

One day when the demon and his hosts come to attack, all of a sudden with a tremendous sound, there appeared a pit in the ground in front of the Linga and Shiv in his dreadful form appeared in that pit. His fiery gaze incinerated Dooshan to ashes as Shiva roared with a tremendous sound. Thus Dooshan was killed and all his cohorts fled in panic. The four brahmana brothers were delighted and sang hymns to placate Shiv's foul temper. Then they prayed him that the deity might aways remain present at that place and Shiv agreed. Since then it is believed that Shiv always remains present in the temple of Mahakala.

(iv) Vindhya And Omkara

Omkar or Omkareshwar is the famous holy spot near Indore, which has the fourth Jyotirlinga. The story about its emergence is given below.

Narada, the divine sage had access to the entire universe. Once he decided to visit Vindhya mountain. The mountain appearing in a human form very reverentially then, welcomed the sage, offering him so many edibles and drinks. Narada was delighted to receive such a warm welcome. He praised the Vindhya mountain for the rich herbs, fruits and herbs available in it range. This made the mountain some what proud, so he said:

"Divine sage, what I have offered to you is nothing compared to what I have. In fact I am full of all the desirable objects that one can even think of."

"Perhaps," replied Narada "But Mount Sumeru is superior to you since it is a favourite mount of the gods who are always available there."

Vindhya felt somewhat downcast. So he decided to become equal of Sumeru in every respect. He began to pray Lord Shiva. For six months he kept on performing devout penance to please Lord Shiv. Eventually pleased with his worship, Shiv appeared before the mountain. Vindhya desired that the Lord may always be present there so that he might become equal of the mount Sumeru. Shiv departed saying : "So be it."

Since that the mountain of Vindhya became also Shiv's favourite and he remains ever present in that temple of Omkareshwara. Omkareshwara means the Lord of the holy syllale of 'ॐ' or Omkar.

It is a combination of the three holy sounds 'a' 'u' and 'm' which control the three super Deities of the Trinity, Viz: Brahma, Vishnu and Mahesh (Shiv).

(v) Kedarnath And Naranarayana

Kedar, the holy seat of Lord Shiv, near Badrinath has the fifth of the Jyotirlingas. It is situated near the twin hills called Nara and Narayana symbolically representing the two holy sages believed to be the incarnate form of lord Vishnu thus two sages prayed for a long time in the hermitage called Badrikashrama. The Kedar peak is nearby.

It was here that the two sages, Nara and Narayana had performed a devout penance to have Lord Shiv before them.

When Shiv appeared he said : "I don't understand why should you two be worshipping me? In fact you both have attained such a pious status that it is you both who should be worshipped.

Anyway, since you have been praying to me for such a long time, let me grant you a boon. I shall ever remain present here." Eversince then Shiv remains present in Kedara.

(vi) Bhimshankara

The sixth Jyotirlinga is at Bhimshankara.

From the Holy Ramayana we know all about Rama and Ravana. Rama it was who not only killed the demon lord Ravana but his brother Kumbhakarana as well. The story about this Jyotirlinga has a direct allusion to some characaters of the Ramayana as well.

There was a demon-woman (Rakshasi) named Karkati who used to live on the mount called Sahya (Sahajadri). She had been married to Kumbhakarana and her son was named Bhim. One day Bhim asked Karkati : "Mother, whose son am I? Why do we live alone in this forest.

Karkati replied: "Listen son, the reason is enshrined in this story. Earlier, before my marriage to your father, Kumbhakarana, I was married to the Rakshasa called Viradha. After his death Kumbhakarana came here and married me. Then you were born. Your father had promised me to take me to Lanka. But soon he was also killed by Rama. With the result, I could never visit Lanka. Since I had no where to go, I started living here and still doing. Where could I have taken you to?"

Bhim was not only sorry to know the cause of his languishing in the jungle but also angry at the god, particular Vishnu whose incarnation was Rama.

"I must take revenge against Rama for his slaying my father and my mother's first husband." with this resolve for a thousand years he prayed to Brahma with his hands raised up to the sky. Constrained by the efficiency of Bhim's devout worship, Brahma appeared before him.

Bhim asked the boon: "Creator ! make me very strong so that I may settle the old scores" Brahma granted this boon.

Now he started searching for Vishnu's devout devotees to vent his spleen against them. This, he thought, was the surest way to force Vishnu come before him. His first target was the king of Kama roopa. Bhim attacked the king and stole all that he possessed. Eventually he conquered his kingdom and imprisoned the king along with his wife. Then he proceeded to conquer the rest of the world.

Meanwhile, in the prison the king and his wife started to pray Lord Shiv. The guards keeping a watch over the royal pair's activities quickly informed Bhim about the devotion the royal couple had started showing towards shiva. Then Bhim decided to kill both of them. As he entered the prison he found the king praying before Shiv linga. When Bhim raised his sword to slay the king, all of a sudden Shiv appeared from the linga and repelled the sword with his trident. Now, Whatever weapon Bhim used, it was repelled and eventually destroyed by Shiv's trident. Finally Shiv slayed Bhim and all his demon cohorts.

The gods who were watching this duel were delighted at the death of yet another demon emerging as a deadly threat to them. When Bhim was killed the gods prayed Shiv that he might always remain present at the spot in the form of the linga. That place is now renowned as Bhimshankar. It is in Kamaroopa district in Assam.

(vii) Vishwanath And Varanasi

The seat of Shiv's seventh Jyotirlinga is in Kashi or Varanasi, the most hallowed place for the devotees of Shiv.

Kashi is also called eternal city. It is so ancient that creator Brahma himself had performed a very difficult 'tapasya' at the conclusion of which he also performed ten Ashwamedha Yagya (the

Horse's sacrifice) which is believed to be a ceremony undertaken only after one gets one's desired success. The Purana claims that it was as difficult a Penance that learning about which Vishnu shook his head in disbelief. When Vishnu did so. One of the jewels from his ear-ring fell down. The place where the 'Moti' (jewel) fell is called Manikarnika Ghat. It is said that one who dies here has his soul going fetter-free to Vaikunth-the realm of Lord Vishnu.

How it became Shiv's favourite seat also has an intersting legend. Once Shiv and Parvati happened to visit Lord Brahma's realm. As the eternal couple entered the realm, Brahma began to hymn his glories from all the five mouths. But one of the mouths committed a mistake in mightly pronouncing a word. This angered Shiv and Shiv severed his one of the faces with a gaze of his third eye . The offending head, though, was severed, it didn't fall on the ground and got stuck up on Shiv's back. The reason was that even though Brahma lost his one head, it amounted to committing the crime of slaying a brahmana, which is believed to be the most heinous sin by the Hindu jurispendence. Hence Shiv had to atone for it.

Shiv himself was helpless since the hacked-off head of Brahma would not come off no matter where he went. This way he kept moving all over the world but that stigma of a 'Brahma-hatya' would not leave him. Eventually he happened to come to kashi. And lo and behold, that severed head of Brahma automatically fell away from Shiv's back. Shiv was delighted to have come to this so holy a place where one even gets absolved of the consequence of committing the most heinous crime. So he decided to remain here. It is due to his grace that kashi is not destroyed even during the Pralaya [Final Dissolutions] because during that period Shiv provides it the support of his trident. When the effect of dissolution subsides he replaces the city at its appointed place. Hence Varanasi is believed to be the holiest place in the world. Lord Shiv is ever present here and any prayer to him gets its earliest responce only in this hallowed city.

(viii) Trymbaka and Gautama

Trymbaka is the hallowed holy tirtha in south of India (Aryavarta) situated on the banks of the river Godavari. It has the eighth Jyotirlinga. The story of its emergence on the map of holy tirthas of the country is given below:

Among the southern mountain ranges there is a mountain peak called Brahma parvata. Eons ago there dwelt the holy sage Gautama with his wife called Ahilya. There the couple had performed a very diffcult tapasya for ten thousand years. But during that period there had occurred a severe draught when it didn't rain for about a 100 years. With the result, there was great shortage of water all over the place, causing death to thousands of living beings. Looking at the sorry plight, Gautama prayed to Varuna, the god of waters on the earth to help them. Varuna appeared at the conclusion of his worship by the sage Gautama and asked him to get a boon.

Gautama said, "Please grant us the boon-that it might rain here," praying to the deity hand-bound.

"Sorry, I can't do this," replied Varuna.

"That is beyond my powers. It is our lord Indra's duty to arrange for rain." Pausing a bit, he further said. "Ask for something which may be with in my powers."

"Then allow us to have a pond here that may be permanently full of water."

Since this Varuna could ensure, a pond of such nature was instantly created. This was a big relief to that drought-torn area and other sages also started to use the pond's water to fulfill their needs. This created a little confusion. Normally Gautama used to send his disciples to fetch water from the pond. But the disciples began to complain that the wives of other sages were creating obstruction and not allowing them to have water. Where upon Ahilya decided to go there to the pond to get water for the hermitage herself.

As she started doing that the wives of the other sages were annoyed and in anger they began to pester Ahilya but she never reacted. These wives then complained to their husbands about Ahilya and Gautama. At first the sages didn't listen but eventually they were convinced that Ahilya and Gautam were wicked and selfish. They therefore sought to hatch a play so that Gautama and Ahilya be punished. In order to achieve their this aim they began to pray Lord Ganesh.

Eventually Ganesh appeared and the sages requested him. "Please grant us this boon that Gautama and Ahilya might be banished from the area."

Lord Ganesh realised that it was an unfair boon since it was Gautama and Ahilya whose efforts had that pond created But he decided to grant them boon because he realised that this could be a good pritense to have the other sages and their wives punished. After all the offenders were they and not Gautama or Ahilya, So, with this thought, Ganesh granted the boon.

The sage Gautama also had some fields of paddy and glain. Ganesh immediately adopted the form of a lean and enervated cow and in that form began to eat up the crop from Gautama's fields. Gautama tried to shoo away the cow with a blade of grass. But as soon as he struck the cow with the blade of grass, the cow, weak and starving as it was, fell down and died. Now, this was a terrible happening. It was a big sin to kill a cow.

Cousequently, other sages combined to force Gautama and Ahilya to leave the hermitage for good. They had no go but to go away and set up an ashrama far away. The other sages completely dissociated themselves from Gautama and Ahilya.

Sage Gautama was quite disturbed with the turn-out of the events. He began to think as to how he should atone to get redemption from the curse of being a cow-slaughter. The sages said. "This could only be possible if you make a round of the earth and then perform a most taxing penance for an entire month. Following this you will have to circle Brahmaparvata a hundred times and bathe in a hundred pots of water. Only then you could be able to get redemption froms this sin."

Gautama and Ahilya performed all the tasks very devotedly, while all the time praying to Lord Shiv.

Eventually Shiv appeared and on the couple's request granted the boon that henceforth the pious river Ganga would be ever present near their hermitage. But Ganga herself raised a condition that her presence near the hermitage must be preceded with Shiv and Parvati also remaining ever present there. Parvati and Shiv agreed to do this. Thus was established Trymbaka, the eighth Jyotirlinga. The river Ganga which flowed there came to be known as Godavari which is still reckoned as 'the Ganga of south India'. Hence the situation of Trymbaka on the bank of Godavari.

Meanwhile, on the recommendation of Gautama and Ahilya the wicked sages were also pardoned by Shiv, after they had performed

the penance by circling the mount Bahmaparvata a hundred times.
Ever since then Lord Shiv is supposed to be ever present in Trymbaka.
It is also called Trymbakeshwar Mahadeva, a holy spot near modern
Nasik.

(ix) Vaidyanath Dham and Ravana

The ninth of the Jyotirlinga is at Vaidyanath Dham. How it
appeared is an interesting tale behind it.

Ravana the renowned demon-lord of the Ramayana fame was
an ardent devotee of Lord Shiv. Once, in order to please his chosen
deity, he went to the Himalayas. He started his worship of the Lord
right from Kailash, the renowned seat of Shiv, but Shiv didn't appear
before him. Then he went to a place a little towards the south called
Vrikshkhandaka. He kept on praying there but again Shiv didn't
appear before him. A hit charged at his failure to please Shiv, Ravana
dig a pit in the earth and started to pray after sitting inside the pit.
There he also established a Shiv linga but still Shiv failed to appear
before him.

This constant failure made Ravana so much desperate and
despondent that he decided to immolate himself. As we all know he
is described to be having as many as ten heads. He lit a fire and
severing his heads, prepared to offer them one by one to the raging
fire. When he had offered his nine heads to the fire and was about to
offer the tenth one, lo and behold, Lord Shiv appeared before him.

"Enough of this, O Demon-Lord." said the Lord of the universe
(Shiv).

"I am satisfied with your worship. You may have your boon
now!"

"Please make me the strongest person of the mortal world and
kindly restore my nine heads to their original position,"

Shiv readily obliged him with this boon.

Then the demon-lord again said." If you are really pleased with
me, then, allow me to carry your symbol from Kailash to Lanka."

Before Shiv could respond to it the divinities conspired to have
Ravana modify his demand. They requested Shiv to put forth a
condition before accepting Ravana's this demand.

Shiv said : "You may take my emblem from Kailash to Lanka
only on one condition. Promise that you will not place it on the earth

anywhere midway your journey. For then, it would become so heavy that you won't be able to lift it."

Ravana, confident after having received the boon of being the strongest person on the earth, thought that he would be able to carry this emblem non-stop to the destination. So he accepted the condition.

As he lifted the Lord Shiv's emblem at Kailash and began to move through the aerial route to Lanka, the gods were concerned and perplexed. They knew that if that Linga happened to get placed in the demons' crtadel at Lanka, that citadel of the demons would become invincible. So they goaded Varuna to enhance the water quantity inside the demon lord's body as much as to make him urinate. This Varuna could do easily.

Meanwhile, when Ravana had crossed not even a few hundred miles from Kailash, he felt an uncontrollable urge to urinate. But he knew that he was not allowed to place the emblem on the earth mid-way. And it would have been tentamount to committing a felonyhad he pissed while carrying the emblem. Desperatily he looked around to find some one to hold the emblem for a few seconds. Immediately he spotted the divine sage Narada loitering thereabout. He accosted him:

"Narada ! Please hold this emblem till I return in a few seconds time." Narada, who had come there out of a divine plot to hoodwink Ravana into breaking the condition set forth by Shiv, Said:

"Well ! Demon-Lord ! I am too feeble to hold it." When Ravana insisted that he would be through in a few seconds time, Narada accepted the emblem.

When Ravana returned after evacuating his bladder, he found Narada standing sheepishly close to the emblem which was placed on the ground. Ravana thundered : " Hey you fool of a sage? Why did you put it on the ground when I had given specific orders to keep it aloft in your hands?"

Narada : "Well ! I told you. I am not that sturdy to hold the emblem of the lord of the universe. It was too heavy to carry. So I put it down. But you are sturdy enough to lift it again."

Then Ravana repeatedly tried to lift the emblem but all in vain. Shiv had already warned him about this possibility. At last, saying his prayer he dejectedly went back to Lanka. The place where that emblem was put at was Vaidyanath dham. This place is in Bihar. Where pouring over this emblem Ganga water during this month of Shrawan is held to be a most consecrated act by the dovotees of Shiv. Since Ravana had ensured that Shiv would ramain ever present in that enblem, it became a Jyotirlinga.

(x) Nagesha

Shiv's tenth Jyotirlinga is at the place called Nagesha. How it came to be in existence is enshrined in a tale given below.

Once upon a time there lived a demon (Rakshasa) called Daruka. His wife's name was Daruki. They dwelt in a forest on the coast of the western sea. Once Daruki had propitiated Goddess Parvati by her devout worship and earned a boon from the Goddess that wherever Daruki went the forest in which she dwelt would inevitably accompany her. Since this forest became a sort of the citadel for the demon pair they began to oppress the world. They destroyed the holy yagya and killed the righteous people adhering to Vedic norms of worshipping the gods, cow and brahmana. People were greatly distressed and in desperation they reported the matter to a powerful sage named Ourva. They requested the sage that he alone could save the world from the iniquities being perpetuated by the wicked demon couple. The sage, Ourva, was eneraged listening about the reign of terror le loose by the demon couple and cursed, Daruka and Daruki that should they commit any more violent act on the earth they would immediately perish.

When the gods and the noble persons learnt about this curse they began to attack the demons. Now the demons were in a great dilemma. In case they didn't fight, the gods would kill them and if they did, owing to the sage Ourva's curse they would die. Eventually they decided to slide down to the base of the ocean where they expected to be safe. Owing to the boon their queen Daruki had received , the whole of the jungle descended down to the ocean base. Since then the ocean became the citadel of the demons. They didn't return to earth. But they still troubled the earth dwellers who travelled by boats to cross the ocean on their business errands.

Once a Vaishya (a member of the trading class) was kidnapped by them. He was a staunch devotee of Lord Shiv. He set up a linga in the prison and began to worship his chosen deity through his this image. when the demons saw the vaishya continuing his worship of Lord Shiv, they began to attack him. His name was Supriya. Seeing his ardent devotee seiged by the wicked demons, Shiv gave him his deadly weapon called Pashupati Astra. With this mighty weapon the Vaishya killed the demons. Seeing their facing total extinction, on the request from Daruki, Goddess Parvati intervened and the remaining demons were saved by the Goddess's intervention. The linga that Supriya worshipped in Nagesha which is a small place near modern Baroda.

XI. Rama And Rameshwara

When Ravana, the demon lord abducted Sita, Rama with his brother Lakshmana and the monkeys and bears managed to reach the end of southern most point of Aryavarta. Now they were confronted with the vast ocean beyond which was the island of Lanka. Sita was held captive in. The problem was how to cross this ocean and reach Lanka. There was neither any bridge nor they had other means to cross the ocean. While Rama was trying to decide how to cross the ocean, he felt very thirsty. He, therefore, requested the monkeys to fetch him some water. But when the water was procured, Rama realised that he shouldn't drink the water without first praying to Shiv.

In order to do so, Rama constructed the linga of Shiv with the help of the sand lying on the shore in abundance. Then he worshipped it with many fragrant flowers. Such were the power of Rama's prayers that not only Shiv but Parvati and her other companions appeared before Rama. Shiv blesssed Rama and Rama requested him to remain ever present in that Linga. The temple housing this Jyiotirlinga is a very hallowed spot for the devotees of Shiv. It is on the far end of the Indian peninsula, at the very tip of it.

(xii) Ghushneshwar and Ghushna

This twelfth Jyotirlinga of Shiv is near modern Daulatabad close to Hyderabad. The tale related to emergance of this linga is as follows:

A brahman named Sudharma used to live near a mountain peak deep in the south called Deva. His wife's name was Sudeha. The couple was of very pious and righteous nature, ever indulged in the worship of various gods. Although they were reasonably well off, they had just one complaint. They had no son. Sudeha, the wife, was especially perturbed on this account. Deeming her to be barren other women used to hurt her with their incisive remarks. "Look-- there goes the barren woman---" they would say: "protect yorself from even her shadow lest it destroys your whole family---" to those that had sons.

Sudharma was also disturbed seeing her wife's condition. One day he decided to conduct an experiment. He plucked two flowers and offered them in front of a sacred fire. Mentaly he associated one of the flowers with having a son and he asked her wife to choose one of the flowers. Unfortunately, his wife chose the flower that was not associated with having a son. This divination scheme's result convinced Sudharma that he was not destined to have a son. But Sudeha refused to be consoled and continued to feel quite miserable.

One day, at last she asked her husband: "Why don't you marry again? Perhaps other wife will beget a son for us. I suggest now you marry my niece Ghushna."

"No, " replied Sudharma : "You love her now because she is your niece. But once she is married to me and gives me a son you will become jealous of her. Then you may start hating her."

But Sudeha managed to convincve her husband that this would never happen. Eventully Sudharma married Ghushna.

Ghushna was a great devotee of Lord Shiv. Everyday she would make a hundred and one lingas out of clay and would worship them. When the day's prayers were over, she would immerse the lingas in a pond. When one lakh of such lingas were immersed in that holy pond, Ghushna became plegnent and in due time gave birth to a hansoms boy. Getting propitiated by Ghushna's worship Lord Shiv decided to fulfil her great desire.

But as soon as she became the proud mother a son, Sudeha became jealous of her, as had been predicted by her husband Sudharna. She thought that her husband was now giving more importance to Ghushna than to her. She felt as though she was being treated like a lowly maid in the house. These thoughts made Sudherna almost insane with jealousy, so much so, that one day she got up in the middle of the night and slew Gushna's son. Then she threw the dead body inside

71

the pond in which Ghushna used to immerse her venerated linga's before.

Meanwhile, unaware of the tragedy, Ghushna woke up early in the morning and as was her everyday ritual she made a linga and began to worship it devoutly. But inside home blood was discovered on the bed yet the newly born boy could not be found anywhere. While everyone else raised the alarm in the house, Ghushna was not distracted by this condition and countinued with her prayer. Lord Shiv was so much impresed with Ghushna's concentration in devotion to him that he restored her son back to life. Not only that, the Lord also wished to kill the wicked lady Sudeha with his trident. But Ghushna begged for her aunt's life and Shiv at last conceded to his devotee's request. This act of forgiveness to her son's murderer further impressed Shiv and he decided to give Ghushna another boon part from restoring her son and filling her coffess with riches and affluence of all kinds.

Ghushna, then asked for a second boon : that the Lord might always remain present in the linga near the pond. Hence the name Ghushneshwra to this 12th Jyotirlinga.

❑❑

17.

Other Important Teerthas of Shiv

(i) Nandikeshwara Teertha

Literally a teertha is the holy spot on the bank of a river but generally it is considered any holy spot. Nandikeshwar teerth also has a most consecrated linga though it is not one of the jyotirlinga. The story of its emergence is given below.

There used to live a brahmana in a city named Karnaki . Once leaving his two sons with his wife he went to visit kashi. It was subsequently learnt that the brahman had died in Kashi. His widow with a great deal of courage and resilience managed to bring her sons up and eventually also married them off. Even when she had herself become very old and emaciated, death continued to elude her. Though daily she prayed, death would not come to her. Her condition had become quite miserable but death didn't come to relieve her of her all afflictions. Suddenly it dawned upon the sons that perhaps their mother was hankering after something and would not die till her that wish was satisfied. One day they asked her directly.

"Mother ! what is that you still desire?"

"Sons ! I have always wanted to visit Kashi," she replied : "So it seems I will not die till I visit Kashi ! But now I am too old to travel to such a long distance. Now you both promise me that when I am died you will take my ashes to Kashi and throw it in the holy river, Ganga."

"This we'll surely do," replied the sons.

"Now you can die in peace."

Soon the mother died and the sons performed her funeral ceremony. Then the eldest son, named Suvadi, set out for Kashi with his mother's ashes. Since the journey was long, he had to travel for the night and rest in a Brahmana's house.

Since it was almost sun-set time when Suvadi reached the brahmana's place, the brahmana came out to milk the cow. But Suvadi saw that when the brahmana tried to milk the cow, the calf created much disturbance as much as to prevent the brahmana from milking the cow. In its anger the calf also kicked the brahmana. Enraged the brahmana also hit the calf with a stick and then quietly milked the cow.

But when the Brahamana left, Suvadi was still there and he was amazed to hear the cow tell its calf : "I am solely disturbed that the brahmana struck you, dear, with a stick. Let him come tomorrow for milking me and I shall be goring him to death."

Next day the cow fulfilled its vow to its calf and gored the brahmana to death when he tried to milk the cow. But this meant that though she was herself a pious animal, it had killed the brahmana which is the most deadly sin. In the heat of the sin's fire the cow, though white, instantly turned black.

The cow then left the house, followed by Suvadi, amazed at the strong happening behind by him. The cow straight away went to the banks of the river Narmada, to the place called Nandikeshwra. As soon as she bathed in the river near that spot, she regained her original colour, sparkling white. This, Suvadi deduced, meant that the stigma of the sin of killing a brahmana was completely washed away by the holy waters of the river Narmada. Suvadi was amazed and the relisation soon dawned upon him that this teertha must be most powerful since it could wash away the deadly sin in a trice. He decided to bathe in that river before setting out to Kashi. As he was bathing there a beautiful woman accosted him. "Where are you going Suvadi." asked the woman. "To throw my mother's ashes into the holy Ganges at Kashi.

"Throw them here only "advised the woman. "This is a far greater 'teertha' than even Varanasi " the woman explained.

"But who are you," asked amazed Suvadi, "I 'm the river Ganga," came the reply. Saying so the woman vanished and Suvadi followed her advice. As soon as he did so his dead mother appeared in the sky and told him that she was fully satisfied. 'Now I will ascend straight to heaven," she said and vanished.

74

. Nandikeshwar is such a soul releasing pious teertha because long ago a brahmana woman named Rishika had performed a great penance at that spot to please Lord Shiv. Since then Nandikeshwar has come to be reckoned as a very holy and hallowed spot for the devotees of Shiv.

(ii) Atreeshwar Teertha

Long ago there was a forest named Kamada. Once it didn't rain there for about hundred years. With the result the trees got withered and dried offering no substitute to the dwellers. So they had no option to quit it for greener pastures.

Seeing this condition, the high sage Atri decided that he would meditate there and pray devoutly to make Indra shower rains in this region.

Sage Atri's wife Anusuiya was as much determined a person as the sage was. So she also decided to perform the difficult penance to please the rain god in the company of her husband. Both of them began to very devoutly pray to Lord Shiv whom they thought to be the ultimate authority to ensure the world's welfare. So difficult was the penance they chose to complete that, it became difficult to decide as to who among them was more determined. Fifty four years passed and they kept on meditating without eating or drinking anything.

Atri's meditation was finally over as he felt mentally that Shiv would care for this forest. But as he rose from his meditation pose, he felt thirsty. He, therefore,asked his wife to go and fetch some water so that he might quench his thirst. While Anusuiya was going to fetch the water, the holy river Ganga appeared before her.

"I am pleased with your dedicated penance," said Ganga. "What boon do you desire ? "

"If you are really happy with me," replied Anusuiya, "please make a pond here and fill the pond with your water. " Ganga readily obliged Ansuiya who filled her water-pot from the pond and brought the water to her husband.

Atri was delighted to drink this water which to him appeared the tastier drink that be had ever inbibed. When he asked Anusuiya why this was so, she told him all that had transpired. Atri, felt curious enough to go to the pond with his wife. They then requested Ganga river to remain ever-present in that pond. Ganga agreed to stay on provided Anusuiya handed over to Ganga all the religious merit (Punya) that she latter had acquired by performing this difficult Tapasya for one year. Anusuiya readily parted with her punya to tempt Ganga stay there eternally.

Meanwhile Shiv was observing this highly noble act on the part of Anusuiya who readily parted with her earned religious merit for the sake of ensuring welfare to the beings of the forest. He quickly appeared before Anusuiya to grant her a boon. Anusuiya and Atri desired a boon that henceforth Shiv might remain ever present in that Kadama forest. Here Shiv is called Atrishwar Mahadeva.

❏❏

18.

The Encounter of Arjuna With Shiv

The Pandavas were passing their days in exile having been robbed of their rightful share in the Hastinapur kingdom by the wicked Duryodhan through a deceitful game of dice. Once these exiled sons of Raja Pandu were resting in a jungle with their common wife Draupadi, when the great sage Vedavyasa reached near them and advised them to pray Shiv. Since Arjuna, the third Pandava was the most brilliant warrior among them, Vedvyasa picked him for performing a devout worship of Lord Shiv. He also told Arjuna a secret Mantra (incantation), which was quite efficacious to please Lord Shiv early. Then he asked Arjuna to go to Mount Indrakila and perform Shiv's worship with total devotion. This mount, among the Himalayas, was situated on the bank of the holy river Bhagirathi.

Arjuna went there and made a small linga for his worship of Lord Shiv. Then he started to perform daily puja of the lord chanting the Shloka he was given by the great sage Vedvyas. While chanting the 'Shloka' he would stand on hours together only on one leg. This way his worship continued. The story of Arjuna performing this difficult Tapasya spread far and wide with many persons growing curious about it. But undanted by the onlookers and other distractions he kept on making strenuous effort to please Shiv.

One day, early in the morning when Arjuna began his worship, all of a sudden a boar approached close to him. In order to end the possibility of his getting distracted, he drew a long arrow from his quiver, set it on to his bow and shot it aiming at the boar. But as his arrow hit the boar in the front Arjuna also heard a noise as if the bear was struck by another arrow on its bindside. Arjuna saw a hunter smiling, standing a few yards away from the prey. But soon a dispute arose as to who had killed the boar. While Arjuna claimed it to be his, the hunter said that it was his prey as his arrow had killed it Since the dispute could not be resolved both of them took their weapons in hand and began to hurl them at each other. To Arjuna's great surprise that hunter easily cut the arrows shot by Arjuna. "Who it could be?" Arjuna was bewildered. "I don't think anybody else except Lord Shankar could be so expert an archer as to cut the arrows shot by Arjuna." Then he mentally concentrated his mind on Lord Shankar and offered some flowers on to the linga before shooting his next arrow. And lo and behold, he found those flowers on the head of that hunter. Arjuna immediately recognised who his adversary was and quickly throwing his bow and arrows aside, he fell flat at the hunter's feet who was no one else but Lord Shiv himself in disguise. Then Shiv appeared in his usual form and raised Arjuna up to press him to his heart. Arjuna said: "Forgive me, O Lord, for my temerity to pick a quarrel against you."

"Don't worry, Arjuna, the best archer," said Shiv. "You may have your boon from me for which you were invoking me all this while"

Arjuna wanted the boon that he might obtain glory on earth. "So be it ," saying, Shiv also handed over to him his famous 'Pashupati astra' which couldn't be cut by any weapon. The possession of this weapon made Arjuna invincible on the earth.

◻◻

19.
How Vishnu Acquired
Sudarshan Chakra

We all know that the deadly discus shaped weapon, the Chakra Sudershana, is Lord Vishnu's renowed weapon, It is said to be such effective a weapon that it never missed its target and always returned to Vishnu after killing or hitting the target. This wonderful weapon had come in to Vishnu's possession out of Lord Shiv's grace. The tale recounting the details is given below.

Eons ago, as usual, the divinities were once greatly troubled by the demon who threw them out of their realm. The gods had to pray to Vishnu for deliverane from this plight. But Vishnu said that only if Lord Shiv could be drawn out of their meditation that they might learn the way to trounce the demons. Then on Gods' advice Vishnu himsef went to Kailash and pray to Shiv. But no matter how deeply he concentrated to invoke Shiv he got no response from the other side. He chanted all the 'Mantras' and Shlokas that were known to please Shiv but to no effect. At last he started the especial devotion to Lord Shiv by chanting the 1000 names dedicated to the latter. At the completion of the chanting every day he would complete his worship by offering a 1000 lotus flowers to the emblem of Shiv. This,too, had continued for some days.

At last, shiva was propitated. But he wanted to test Vishnu's devotion to him. So, when one day, the chanting of the 1000 names was over, he stole one lotus flower from the 1000 flowers kept there to complete the worship formally. Shiv quietly took that flower away. When Vishnu found one lotus flower missing, he thought : "all say that my eyes look like fresh lotus flowers, when shouldn't I gouge out one of them to make good the loss." Thinking this way he gouged out one of his eyes and offered it alongwith the 999 lotus flowers. Shiv was now immensely pleased with Vishnu and appeared before him. He offered to grant Vishnu a boon.

"Lord give me such a mighty weapon as may never be destroyed and it may never miss its target. I need it to fight demons with." Vishnu requested.

Shiv immediately procured this Sudershan Chakra and, offering it to Vishnu, said : "Take this weapon, It shall always return to you after completing the assigned task, "Vishnu gratefully accepted it and killed the demons soon.

□□

20.

Thousand Names of Lord Shiva

Many eons ago, a fierce war raged between the gods and the demons. The gods received a sound thrashing and fled. While they were running away, they happened to encounter Vishnu. When Vishnu asked the reason and learnt about it, he advised the gods to start praying Lord Tripurari (Shiva) since "only he is capable of subduing these wroth demons". Then saying so Vishnu also joined the gods to invoke Lord Shiva to their presence. Guided by Lord Vishnu they chanted the 1000 names of Lord Shiva. [For convenience all these 1000 names have been grouped in the categories containing 10 names each]. These names are:

1. Gunakaraga, Satyasatyapara, Dina, Dharmaga, Ananda, Dharmasadhana, Anantadrishti, Danda, Damayita, Dama.
2. Abhivadva, Mahamaya, Vishvakarma, Visharada, Vitaraga, Vinitama, Tapasvi, Bhutabhavana, Unmattavesha, Pracchanna.
3. Jitakama, Ajitapriya, Kalyanaprakriti, Kalpa, Sarvalokaprajapati, Tarasvi, Tavaka, Dhimana, Pradhanaprabhu, Avyaya.
4. Lokapala, Antarhitatma. Kalpadi. Kamallekshana, Vedashastrarthatattvajna. Aniyama. Niyatashraya. Chandra. Surya, Shani.
5. Ketu, Varanga, Vidrumaacchavi, Bhaktivashya, Anagha, Parabrahmamrigavanarpana, Adri, Adryalaya, Kanta, Paramatma.
6. Jagadguru, Sarvakarmalaya, Tushta, Mangalya, Mangalavrita, Mahatapa, Dirghatapa, Sthavishtha, Sthavira, Dhruva.

7. Aha, Samvatsara, Vyapti, Pramana, Paramatapa, Samvatsarakara, Mantrapratyayakara, Sarveshvara, Aja, Sarvadarshana.

8. Siddha, Mahareta, Mahabala, Yogi, Yogya, Siddhi, Mahateja, Sarvadi, Agraha, Vasu.

9. Vasumana, Satya, Sarvapapahara, Sukirti, Shobhana, Shrimana, Avanmanasagochara, Amritashashvata, Shanta, Vanahasta.

10. Mridu, Samadhivedya, Kodandi, Nilakantha, Parashvadhi, Vishalaksha, Mrigavyadha, Suresha, Suryatapana, Dharmadhama.

11. Kshamakshetra, Bhagavana, Bhaganetrabhida, Data, Dayakara, Bhava, Savagatah, Purusha, Sarva, Arthitavya.

12. Daksha, Karmandi, Kamashasana, Shmashananilya, Suksha, Shmashanastha, Maheshavara, Lokakarta, Mrigapati, Mahakarta.

13. Mahoushadhi, Uttara, Gopati, Gopta, Jnanagmya, Puratana, Niti, Suniti, Shuddatma, Soma.

14. Somarata, Sukhi, Somapa, Amritapa, Soumya, Mahatejah, Mahadyuti, Tejomaya, Amritamaya, Annamaya.

15. Sudhapati, Ajatshatru, Aloka, Sambhavya, Havyavahana, Lokakara, Vedakara, Sutrakara, Sanatana, Maharshi.

16. Kapilcharya, Vishvadipti, Vilochana, Pinakapani, Bhudeva, Svastida, Svastikrita, Sudhi, Dhatridhama, Dhamakara.

17. Sarvaga, Sarvagochara, Brahmasrika, Vishvasrika, Sarga, Karanikara, Priya, Kavi, Shakha, Vishakha.

18. Goshakha, Shiva, Bhishaka, Anuttama, Gangaplavodaka, Bhavya, Pushkala, Sthapati, Sthira, Vijitatma.

19. Vishayatma, Bhutavahana, Sarathi, Sagana, Ganakaya, Sukirti, Chinnasamshaya Kamadeva, Kamapala, Bhasmoddulita-vigraha.

20. Bhasmapriya, Bhasmashayi, Kami, Kanta, Kritagama, Samavarta, Nivritatma, Dharmapunja, Sadashiva, Akalmasha.

21. Chaturvahu, Durvasa, Durasada, Durlabha, Durgama, Durga, Sarvayudhavisharada, Adhyatmayoganilaya, Sutantu, Tanturvardhana.

22. Shubhanga, Lokasaranga, Jagadisha, Janardana, Bhasmashuddhikara, Meru, Ojasvi, Shuddhavigraha, Asadhya, Sadhusadhya.

23. Bhrityamarkatarupadhrika, Hiranyareta, Pourana, Ripujivahara, Bala, Mahahrada, Mahagarta, Vyali, Siddhavrindaravandita, Vyaghracharmambara.

24. Shiva, Hara Mrida, Rudra, Pushkara, Pushpalochana, Arthigamya, Sadachara, Sharva, Shambhu.

25. Maheshvara, Chandrapida, Chandramouli, Vishva, Vishvamareshvara, Vedantasarasandoha, Kapil, Nilalohita, Dhyanadhara, Aparicchedya.

26. Gouribharta, Ganeshvara, Ashtamurti, Vishvamurti, Trivargasvargasadhana, Jnanagamya, Dridaprajna, Devadeva, Trilochana, Vamadeva.

27. Mahadeva, Patu, Parvrida, Drida, Vishvarupa, Virupaksha, Vagisha, Shuchisattama, Sarvapramanasamvadi, Vrishanka.

28. Vrishavahana, Isha, Pinaki, Khatvanga, Chitravesha, Chirantana, Tamohara, Mahayogi, Gopta, Brahma.

29. Dhurjati, Kalakala, Krittivasah, Subhaga, Pranavatmaka, Unnadhra, Purusha, Jushya, Durvasa, Purashasana.

30. Divyayudha, Skandaguru, Parameshthi, Paratpara, Anadimadhyanidhana, Girisha, Girijadhava, Kuberabandhu, Shrikantha, Lokavarnottama.

31. Mahabhuta, Mahanidhi, Amirtasha, Amritavapu, Panchajanya, Prabhanjana, Panchaviṁshatitattvastha, Parijata, Para-uara, Sulabha.

32. Suvrata, Shura, Brahmavedanidhi, Nidhi, Varnashramaguru, Varni, Shatrujita, Shatrutapana, Ashrama, Kshapana.

33. Kshama, Jnanavana, Achaleshvara, Pramanabhuta, Durjneya, Suparna, Vayvahana, Dhanurdhara, Dhanurveda, Gunarashi.

34. Guruda, Lalita, Abheda, Bhavatmatmasamsthita, Vireshvara, Vyavasaya, Vyavasthana, Hara Jagdiya, Param.

35. Virabhadra, Virasanavidhi, Virata, Virachudamani, Vetta, Tivrananda, Nadidhara, Ajnadhara, Trishuli, Shipivishta.
36. Shivalaya, Balakhilya, Mahachapa, Tigmamshu, Badhira, Khaga, Adhirama, Susharana, Subrahmanya, Sudhapati.
37. Maghavana, Koushika, Gomana, Virama, Sarvasadhana, Lalataksha, Vishvadeha, Sara, Samsarachakrabhrita, Amoghadanda.
38. Madhyastha, Hiranya, Brahmavarchasi, Paramartha, Para, Mayi, Shambara, Vyaghralochana, Ruchi, Virinchi.
39. Svarbandhu, Vachaspati, Aharpati, Ravi, Virochana, Skanda, Shasta, Vaivasvata, Yama, Yukti.
40. Unnatakiriti, Sanuraga, Paranjaya, Kailashadhipati, Kanta, Savita, Ravilochana, Vidvattama, Vitabhaya, Vishabharta.
41. Anivarita, Nitya, Niyatakalyana, Punyashravanakirtana, Durashrava, Vishvasaha, Dhyeya, Duhsvapnanashana, Uttarana, Dushkritiha.
42. Vijneya, Duhsaha, Bhava, Anadi, Bhurbhuvakshi, Kiriti, Ruchirangada, Janana, Janajanmadi, Pritimana.
43. Paratapvana, Kamadalundhara, Dhanvi, Vedanga, Vedavita, Muni, Bhrajihnu, Bhojana, Bhokta, Lokantha.
44. Duradhara, Atindriya, Mahamaya, Sarvavasa, Chatushpatha, Kalayogi, Mahanada, Mahotsaha, Mahabala, Mahabuddhi.
45. Mahavirya, Bhutachari, Purandara, Nishachara, Pretachari, Mahashakti, Mahadyuti, Ahiraeshyavapu, Shrimana, Sarvacharyamanogati.
46. Vahushtuta, Niyatatma, Dhruva, Adhruva, Sarvashaska, Ojastejodyutidhara, Nartaka, Nritypriya, Nrityanitya, Prakashatma.
47. Prakashaka, Spashtakshara, Budha, Mantra, Samana, Sarasamplava Yugadikrida, Yugavarta, Gambhira, Vrishavahana.
48. Ishta, Vishishta, Shishteshta, Shalabha, Sharabha, Dhanu, Tirtharupa, Tirthanama, Tirthadrishya, Stuta.
49. Arthada, Apamnidhi, Adhishthana, Vijaya, Jayakalavita, Pratishthita, Pramanajana, Hiranyakavacha, Hari,

Vimochana.

50. Hiranyagarbha, Druhina, Bhutapala, Bhupati, Sadyogi, Yogavit, Yogi, Varada, Brahmanapriya, Devapriya.

51. Devanatha, Devajana, Devachintaka, Vishamksha, Vishalaksha, Vrishada, Vrishavardhana, Nirmama, Nirahamkara, Nirmoha.

52. Nirupadrava, Darpaha, Darpada, Drita, Sarvabhutaparivartaka, Sahasrajit, Sahararchi, Prabhava, Snigddhaprakritidakshina, Bhutabhavyabhavannatha.

53. Bhutinashana, Artha, Anartha, Mahakosha, Parakaryaikapandita, Nishkantaka, Kirtananda, Nirvyaja, Vyajamardana, Sattvavana.

54. Sattvika, Satyakirti, Snehakritagama, Akampita, Gungrahi, Naikatma, Naikakarmakrit, Suprita, Sumukha, Suksha.

55. Sukara, Dakshinanila, Nandiskandhadhara, Dhurya, Prakata, Pritvardhana, Aparajita, Sarvasattva, Govinda, Adhrita.

56. Sattvavahana, Svadhia, Siddha, Putamurti, Yashodhana, Varahabhringadhrika, Bhringi, Balavana, Ekanayaka, Shrutiprakasha.

57. Shrutimana, Ekabandhu, Anekakrit, Shrivatsalashivarambha, Shantabhadra, Sama, Yasha, Bhushaya, Bhushana, Sthanada.

58. Suragana, Vidyesha, Vindusamshraya, Balarupa, Vikarta, Balonmatta, Gahana, Guha, Karana, Karta.

59. Sakala, Nishkala, Anagha, Akala, Sakaladhara, Pandurabha, Mrida, Nata Purna, Purayita.

60. Punya, Sukumara, Sulochana, Samageyapriya, Akrura, Punyakirti, Anamaya, Manojava, Tirthakara, Jatila.

61. Jiviteshvara, Jivitantakara, Nitya, Vasureta, Vasuprada, Sadgati, Satkriti, Siddhi, Sajjati, Kalakantaka.

62. Kaladhara, Mahakala, Bhutasatyaparayana, Lokalavanyakartta, Lokottarasukhalaya, Chandrasanjivana, Shasta, Lokaguda, Mahadia, Lokabandhu.

63. Lokanatha, Kritajna, Krittibhuyshana, Anapaya, Akshara, Kanta, Sarvashastrabhudvara, Tejomaya, Dyutidhara,

Lokagrani.

64. Anu, Shuchismita, Prasannatma, Durjjeya, Duratikrama, Jyotirmaya, Jagannatha, Nirakara, Jaleshvara, Tumbavma.

65. Mahakopa, Vishoka, Shokanashana, Trilokapa, Trilokesha, Sarvashuddhi, Adhokshaja, Avyaktalakshnana, Deva, Vyaktavyakta.

66. Vishampati, Varashila, Varaguna, Saramandhana, Maya, Brahma, Vishnu, Prajapala, Hamsa, Hanmsagati.

67. Vaya, Vedha, Vidhata, Dhata, Srashta, Harta, Chaturmukha, Kailasashikharavasi, Sarvavasi, Sadagati.

68. Unishpanna, Surabhi, Shishiratmaka, Vasanta, Madhava, Grishma, Nabhasya, Vijavahana, Angira, Guru.

69. Atreya, Vimala, Vishvavahana, Pavana, Sumati, Vidvana, Travidya, Naravahana, Manobuddhi, Ahamkara.

70. Kshetrajna, Kshetrapalaka, Jammadagni, Balanidhi, Vigalal, Vishvagalava, Aghora, Anuttara, Yajna, Shreya.

71. Nishreyahpatha, Shaila, Gaganakundabha, Danavari, Arindama, Rajanijanaka, Charuvishalya, Lokakalpadhrika, Chaturveda, Chatrubhava.

72. Chatura, Chaturapriya, Amlaya, Samamlaya, Tirthaveda-shivalaya, Vahurupa, Maharupa, Sarvarupa, Charachara, Nyayanirmayaka.

73. Nyayi, Nyayagamya, Nirantara, Sahasramurddha, Devendra, Sarvashastraprabhanjana, Munda, Virupa, Vikranta, Dandi.

74. Danta, Gunottama, Pingalaksha, Janadhyaksha, Nilagriva, Niramaya, Sahasravahu, Sarvesha, Sharanaya, Sarvalokadhrika.

75. Padmasana, Paramjyoti, Parampara, Paramfala, Padmagarbha, Mahagarbha, Vishvagarbha, Vichakshana, Characharajna, Varada.

76. Varesha, Mahabala, Devasuraguru, Deva, Devaura-mahashraya, Devadideva, Devagni, Devagnisukhada, Prabhu, Devasureshvara.

77. Divya, Devasuramaheshvara, Devadevamaya, Achintya, Devadevatamasambhava, Sadyoni, Asuravyaghra,

Devasimha, Divakara, Vibhudhagravara.

78. Shreshtha, Sarvadevottamottama, Shivajnanarata, Shrimana, Shikhi-Shriparvatapriya, Vajrashasta, Siddhakhadgi, Narasimhanipatana, Brahmachari, Lokachari.

79. Dharmachari Dhandhipa, Nandi, Nandishvara, Ananta, Nagnavratadhara, Shuchi, Lingadhyaksha, Suradhyaksha, Yogadhyaksha.

80. Yugavaha, Svadharma, Svargata, Svargakhara, Svaramayasvana, Vanadhyaksha, Vijakarta, Dharmakrit, Dharmasabhava, Dambha.

81. Alobha, Arthavit, Shambhu, Sarvabhutamaheshvara, Shmashananilaya, Tryksha, Setu, Apratimakriti, Lokottaras-phutaloka, Trymbaka.

82. Nagabhushana, Andhakari, Makhadveshi, Vishnukandharapatana, Dhurjati, Khandaparshu, Papahari, Akarti Hara, Rudra.

83. Nitimana, Dhava, Vasishtha, Kashyapa, Bhanu, Bhima, Bhimaparakrama, Pranava, Salpatchachara, Mahakasha.

84. Mahaghana, Janmadhipa, Mahadeva, Sakalagamaparaga, Tattva, Tattavit, Ekatma, Vibhu, Vishvavibhushana, Rishi.

85. Brahmana, Aishvaryajanmanrityujaratiga, Panchayajnasamutpatti, Vishvesha, Vimalodaya, Atmayoni, Vatsala, Bhaktalokadhrika, Gayatrivallabha, Anayanta.

86. Pramshu, Vishvavasa, Prabhakara, Shishu, Girirata, Samrata, Sushena, Surashatruha, Amogha, Arishtanemi.

87. Kumuda, Vigatajvara, Svayamjyoti, Tanujyoti, Achanchala, Atamajyoti, Pingala, Kapliashmashru, Bhalanetra, Trayitanu.

88. Jnanaskandarnahaniti, Vishvotpatti, Upadlava, Bhaga, Vivasvana, Aditya, Yogapara, Divaspati, Kalyangunanama, Papaha.

89. Punyadarshana, Udarakirti, Udyogi, Sadyogi, Sadasanmaya, Nakshatramali, Divaspati, Nakesha, Svadhishthanapadashraya, Pavitra.

90. Manipura, Nabhogati, Hrit, Pundarikasina, Shatru, Shranta, Vrishakapi, Ushna, Grihapati, Krishna.

91. Paramartha, Anarthanashana, Adharmashatru, Ajneya, Puruhuta, Purushruta, Brahmagarbha, Vrihadgarbha, Dharmadhenu Dhanagama.

92. Jagaddhitaishi, Sugata, Kumara, Kushalagama, Hiranyavarna, Jyotishmana, Nanabhutarata, Dhvani, Araga, Nayanadhyaksha.

93. Vishvamitra, Dhaneshvara, Brahmajyoti, Vasudhama, Mahajyotianuttama, Matamaha, Matarishva, Nabhasvana, Nagaharadhrika, Pulastya.

94. Pulaha, Agastya, Jalukarnya, Parashara, Niravarananirvara, Vairanchya, Vishtarashrava, Atmabhu, Aniruaddha, Atri.

95. Jnananmurti, Mahayasha, Lokaviragrani, Vira, Chanda, Satyaparakrama, Vyalakalpa, Mahakalpa, Kalpaviriksha, Kaladhara.

96. Alankarishnu, Achala, Rochishnu, Vikramonnata, Ayuhshabdapati, Vegi, Plavana, Shikhisarathi, Asamsrishta, Atithi.

97. Shatrupreamathi, Padapasana, Vasushrava, Pratapa, Havyavaha, Vishvabhojana, Japaya, Jaradishamana, Lohitatma, Tanunapata.

98. Vrihadashva, Nabhoyoni, Supratika, Tamisraha, Nidagha, Tapana, Megha, Svaksha, Parapuranjaya, Sukhanila.

99. Vivikshu, Visharada, Shubda, Shubha, Karta, Shubhanama, Shobhan, Anarthita, Ageena, Sakshi.

100. Parathavritti, Nityashantiparayana, Mahatyagi, Satyavrata, Nilalohita, Kaleha, Bhakti Raja, Akampa Bhootabhavana, Bhutakriti.

---

1. It is apparent that some names have been repeated and some are also the epithets used for other super-gods. But some common names have different meanings by Sanskrit grammar which vary according to the context they are used in.

21.
The Story of Vedanidhi

Long Long ago in the city of Avanti (Ujjayani, modern Ujjain) there lived a very righteous brahmana. He was very pious and truthful. He had two sons named Sunidhi and Vedanidhi. The younger son, Vedanidhi was wicked and evil-minded.

The brahmana was also a favourite of the king of Avanti owing to the former's truthful nature and pious conduct. Once the king presented to the brahmana a gold bangle. The brahmana took it home and gave it to his wife for storing it in utter safety. But the wicked son Vedanidhi happened to find about it. He stole it quietly and presented it to a nautch-girl.

As the Providence would have it, one day that dancing girl was called by the king to give her dancing performance. During the show the king happened to recognise that gold bangel which he had given to the pious brahmana. He retrieved that bangle from the dancing girl after the show after compensating her adequately.

Then he summoned the brahamana. "Do you remember that I had given to you a gold bangle? " asked the king "Can you please return it to me? I need it",

The brahmana hurried back home and asked his wife for the bangle. But though she searched the entire day it couldn't be found. Subseqently it was revealed that vedanidhi had stolen it. The brahmana punished his son by banishing him from the house.

Vedanidhi kept on wandering here and there and begged food so that he might eat. One day he didn't get any food. That happened to be the holy day of Shivratri, the day of Shiv's wedding. Vedanidhi was aware of it. He saw several people going to Shiv's temple with

89

all sorts of offerings, including food, in their hands. The evil brahmana thought that he might be able to steal some of the food items and thus might satisfy his hunger. He followed the devotees to the temple and waited till their falling asleep after saying their prayers.

As he found all asleep, Vedanidhi crept up to the place where the offerings had been kept. That spot was exactly before the linga. It was quite dark there and Vedanidhi couldn't see very well. An earthen lamp was burning and the shadow of the lamp fell on the linga. Vedanidhi tore off a piece of cloth from his clothing and stuffed it into the lamp so that it might burn better. This made the flick of the lamp rise higher which removed the shadow falling on to the linga.

However, as Vedanidhi was about to steal the edible items from the offerings, the devotees awoke. Seeing this intruder they gave chase to Vedanidhi and shot many arrows at him. These arrows hit Vedanidhi and he died.

Following his death, Yama's (the death god's) messangers came there to take the soul of Vedanidhi to hell, But Shiv's henchmen also reached there and prevented them from doing so. No matter with what intention, Vedanidhi had kept fast on the day of Shivratri, although unknowingly, stayed awake for the whole night and had also removed the shadow from the linga. These were, actully, the acts that only a most faithful devotee of Shiv is expected to do. Thus Vedanidhi turned into a faithful devotee of Shiv deserving to be taken to the realm of Shiv. This way Vedanidhi's all sins were forgiven and he carved a place in Kailash. Such is Lord Shiv, Very kind and looking to his devotees.

❏❏

22.

The Shivratri Fast : Its Significance

Normally it is heard that Shivratri is the day when Shiv got married to Parvati. However, according to this Purana (Shiv Purana) it is the 'tithi' (llunar day) on which Brahma and Vishnu had worshipped Shiv. Neverthless, the fact cannot be denied that it is the day (or precisely the night) that is dedicated to Shiv's especial worship. The devout keep strict fast on this day. They eat only herbs, fruit and roots and devote entire night in visiting various temples dedicated to Lord Shiv which are especially decorated on this day. The fast bestows on the devotee an undecaying Punya (religious merit). Even if one does so without knowing the significance of it, Lord Shiv remains especially pleased with him. The previous story also highlighted this point, and so does the story of Rurudruha, given below.

There used to dwell a hunter in a certain forest. He was an evil-minded, cruel and wicked person. He would kill even the most hapless being without feeling sorry in the least. Apart from being a hunter be was also a robber and a thief. Naturally he was totally ignorant about the significance of Shivratri.

One day it was the Shivratri day and his family members were starving. Owing to fierce rains on the previous day Rurudruha couldn't find a prey. Since they all were feeling very hungry they forced Rurudruha to go out and arrange a meal for the family members. The hunter went to the forest but couldn't get any pray. He waited for the entire day but to no relief. It was now already dark and no game was to be seen. During his prowling, he happened to spot a water course. He decided to keep a strict vigil there. Sooner or later some amimal was bound to turn up there. In order to be safe from a sudden attack, he decided to wait perched atop a tree. That tree, close to the water-hole, was the 'Bilva' tree, the favourite tree of Lord Shiv. He had also kept a water-pot duly filled up from the pond to avoid going down to the tiny tarn should he feel thirsty later on. Then he waited for any animal to turn up there .

As his good luck would have it, a doe turned up to drink water. The hunter picked up his bow and arrow. But in doing so he shook the tree a bit, but enough to make it shed some leaves down. They fell on the linga which was existing right beneath the tree. The little commontion on the tree also let some water spill out from the waterpot and fall on the linga. Rururuha, of course, was unaware of what he was causing to the tree and to the linga established beneath the tree.

This commotion also allerted the doe and she looked at the hunter. "Don't kill me right now," the doe was seemingly saying to the hunter. "My children and husband are waiting for me at my hide out. Let me go and bid them fare well. When I return you are welcome to kill me."

The hunter, cruel by nature was in no mood to let that doe go. "Does any animal ever return to be killed" he thought. But the doe took an oath and Rurudruha let it go.

After a short while another doe terned up to drink water. The two does were sisters and they were married to the same deer. As before, in taking aim the hunter again shook the tree and in the process lathing some Bilva leaves and water-drops fall on to the linga.

This doe also requested the hunter to let it go and bid farewell to its family members. The hunter was reluctant to let the doe go but he thought: "Well this water hole is drawing enough of preys for me. I may get even a better one. "So when the second doe made the request, the hunter also acceded to it."

As he had expected, this time a deer appeared near the water-hole. And when the hunter picked up his bow and arrow, the 'Bilva' leaves and some water from the water pot fell on the linga again.

The deer said : "Hunter, let me go. I will surely come back soon I wish to say good-bye to my family members.

The deer also took oath that it would return and the hunter, Rurudruha let it go, again.

After some time had passed, two does and one deer returned as they had promised, accompanied by their tiny children. Each said : "Kill me and spare the others. They must stay alive and look after the children. "The babies of the deer family also said : "Kill us and spare out parents. We don't wish to live when they are dead." The hunter was surprised to find them so considerate to each other. He again made some movement in amazement at such self-sacrificing deer-family, which again caused some 'Bilva' leaves and water to fall on the linga beneath. Moreover, the night-long fast, though kept unknowingly, also purified Rurudruha's heart by Shiv's grace. Shiv also took pity on Rurudruha and removed all evil thoughts from the hunter's mind. The hunter eventually spared the entire deer family.

As soon as he did so, Lord Shiv appeared before the hunter and said:

"Yours is now a blessed existence. Hence-forth your name will be Guha. One day Lord Rama will be your guest."

This story emphasises that one gets enough Punya by observing fast and offering Bilva leaves and water to the linga even though one may be doing so unconsciously.

❏❏

23.
Why Shiv's One Epithet Is Chandrashekhar

Once the mother of the world (Jagjanani) Parvati asked the Lord of universe, Shiv : "Lord'! Why do you always wear a crescent moon on your forehead. What's the secret behind this adornment?

Shiv, then, narrated the full story.

After Sati's death in the yagya of Daksha,Shiv was so woebegone and desolate that the fire of the seperation from his wife had started burning the forests and the spots he would maditate in . As he, being disturbed, moved ahead he started carrying vast devastation alongwith him. The earth began to be depleted and what was left was only badly charred earth. Seeing this the gods were greatly alarmed as Shiv's intense grief seemed to ruin the entire creation. They rushed to Brahma and sought his advice. The creator said : His body is affire because of his intense grief. What he needs is something that may cool his temper and provide relief to him." Then he adviced the gods to gift the moon to Shiv which had nectar inside and which was quite soothing to eye. Shiv gratefully placed it on his forehead and felt quite releived from the burning grief. Chandrashekhar means one who has the Chandra (Moon) atop his crown.

❏❏

24.
Why Ash Covers Shiv's Body

Countinuing the discussion, Parvati said: "Now I understand why you have the moon at your forehead? But why do you keep your body ever covered with ash ? What made out choose this most unusual decor."

Shiv smiled detecting the sarcasm and recounted the full episode.

Long ago there used to be a brahamana who was the scion of the great sage Bhrigu's family. So devout and of pious natured he was that he decided to perform a very difficult penance (Tapasya). He would stand unclad in the open in the freezing cold or smouldering summers and wouldn't cover himself even when it rained cats and dogs. He seemed to have an unbreakable concentration. When he felt hungry he will shed even the most wild beasts of the jungle to fetch some fruits. Those wild animals would never attack him due to the divine glow that he had developed and behaved as if they were the pets of the brahamana. He did so for about a hundred years and then stopped eating even fruits. Then he started suviving on the green leaves, earning for himself an epithet 'Parnada' . He continued his tapasya unendingly.

One day while he was cutting some grass to repair his hut, the scythe he was using fell from his hands and sliced off his middle finger. Parnada was amazed to find no blood rushing from the wound on his finger. Instead, a sap (of flowers) like fluid oozed out from it. Now Parnada thought : "I must have became very pios by surviving on fruits and leaves. Hence the sap and not blood issuing out of my wounds," This thought filled enough vanity in his mind, 'I'm the most pious man now." He began to leap with uncontrollable delight.

Seeing a noble person developing vanity, Shiv decided to teach him a lesson to clear his mind from such self-conceited ideas. With this idea, Shiv disguised himself a brahmana and arrived before Parnada.

"Why are you so happy ?" Shiv asked

"Can't you see? " replied Parnada . "My Tapasya has been successful. I'm the most pious man in the world ?"

"How can you say so"? asked the other brahmana.

"You see," Parnada began self conceitedly, "My blood has become as pious as the sap of the fruits and leaves, you cut any part of me and have it in abundance,'

"This sort of vanity destroys the fruit of all tapasya," advised Shiv. "Even then you have nothing deserving your feeling so much elated? Your blood has only turned into the sap of the plants. But what will happen when you burn trees and plants.' Only ash remains that's surely the higher stage. I myself have performed so much 'tapasya' that my blood has become ash-like."

Saying so Shiv sliced off his middle finger and ash came out of it. Parnada was quite impressed. He realised that there was nothing that he could be proud of, here was a far superior a hermit that he. Then he asked the brahmana (Shiv) as to who he actually was and then Shiv revealed his true form before Parnada. Evere since that day ash never leaves Shiv's body.

❑❑

25.
The Story of Nandi

Ages ago there lived a sage called Shilada. Once he saw through his yogic powers that his ancestors were being tortured in hell. When he tried to find out the reason he learnt that this was because of him only. He didn't have a son and hence the family lineage was disturbed. So unless Shilada got a son his ancestors would continue to be tortured in hell.

In order to obtain a son, the sage began the worship of Lord Shiv, the bestower of his devotee's every desired boon. He kept on praying for about a 1000 years through a very difficult Tapasya. Eventually Shiv was pleased. He appeared and offered to grant Shilada the desired boon.

Shilada said : "Lord ! Grant me a boon that may give us a virtuous son". "So be it", the Lord said and disappeaared.

Some days after his receiving this boon when Shilada was ploughing the land, he discorvered a baby boy placed on the plough. The boy was as bright as the sun and fire. Shilada was frightened and tried to run away.

Then he heard a heavenly voice say : "Shilada ! Don't run away. This is the boy that you prayed for. Since this boy would make everyone happy, he has to be called Nandi."

Happily Shilada brought the boy home and began to teach him the Vedas and all that he know : about medicines, dancing and singing, and the sacred texts. The brilliant boy learnt all knowledge in about a fortnight's time only.

When Nandi was about seven years old there arrived two powerful sages at the hermitage of Shilada. Their names were Mitra and Varun, the pair of the most respected seers. Shilada welcomed them very reverentially and after offering choicest fruits etc., he presented Nandi before them. The sages blessed Nandi with "be learned and be faithful to your father."

Shilada objected. "Why don't you bless my son with long life ? He is already quite learned and faithful to me."

The sages explained. "Your this brilliant son will die when he is eight years old. That is orained by his stars."

Hearing this Shilada was quite perturated. But Nandi consoled his father by saying that by devotedly praying to Shiv he would have his destiny rewritten. "For Shiv is the only god who has the power to alter one's destiny."

But Shilada said : "Do you know it may take thousands of years to please Shiv. I had to meditate for a thouasnd year to make him appear and grant the boon of having you as my son. How do you expect to please Shiv and make him appear before you in a year's time that is left to you?"

But the boy was undaunted, "Wait and watch father," he said : "Shiv is difficult to appease if you only perform Tapasya and seek to quench your thirst of knowledge. But he can be pleased in a trice if your faith in him is genuine and devotion unswerving. That is what I have gathered from my study of the holy texts. I am sure, realising the intensity of my feeling he would appear before me soon."

Saying so he left to a river called Bhuvana. Nandi entered this river and began to pray Shiv while still under the water. As Nandi expected he found a smiling Shiv before him in no time.

"What boon do you seek from me, Nandi ?" asked the benign Lord.

"Please grant me the boon that I may be ever devoted to you," Nandi requested."Now I don't want to be born again, become old and die."

Shiv granted this boon to Nandi and added : "Henceforth your father would stay in my realm along with you. You both are now beyond the cycle of births and death." Shiv also made Nandi the Chief of his henchmen, called the 'Ganas' and added the epithet Ganapati to his name. He retained him as his perpetual assistant. Shiv also gave a wonderful garland to Nandi to wear. As soon as Nandi put that garland his body illumiated like a 1000 suns with three eyes raining fire. Eversince then Nandi is Shiv's inseperable companion.

❏❏

26.
How Parvati Became Gauri

Once there emerged two powerful demons called Shumbha and Nishumbha following their dedicated worship of Brahma who granted the duo their desired boon that they would not be killed by males.

On the strength of this boon they became so powerful as to oppress the whole world and drive the gods out of their realm. Distressed, the gods rushed to Brahma to request the creator to offer some solution to the problem.

Brahma said : "Only Shiv can provide you help."

Then on Brahma's advice they prayed to Shiv who appeared there, Brahma said to Shiv : "You have to help the gods. I have given a boon to the demons Shumbha and Nishumbha. Now they have grown very powerful. Since they cannot be killed by males by virtue of that boon, you must produce a dark and deadly female figure from Parvati's body. Only that female could be able to slay these two demons."

Shiv realised the gravity of the problem and said :" I'll try,"

When Shiv reached near Parvati, in quite a non-chalant vein, he addressed her as "Kali" ! Parvati was sorely angry at her husband calling her 'Kali' which means dark complexioned woman or a black woman.

"Why do you address me this way; I'm not 'Kali' but 'Gori' [Fair comlexioned] ". But since Shiv's words could not be false, Parvati, indeed, turned into a black woman.

Now she was most unhappy. She said angrily to Shiv. "If you have my this appearance in your mind., then why did you pretend to love me? Cursed is the life of that woman whose husband carries such derogatory opinon about his espouse."

Then after a pause she declared: "Now I am going to do a difficult 'tapasya' to get back my original colour. I am going to pray Brahma. Now I will meet you only when I become 'Gori'." (Gauri).

With this challenge, Parvati went off to meditate. She remained lost in her tapasya for many years.

While she was meditating, she spotted a tiger sitting in front of her. While she thought it to be one of her devotees sitting there to protect her from the wild beasts, the tiger was really a wicked beast, he was sitting there to eventually gobble her up as its choicest dinner. However, gradually Parvati's assessment of the tiger's nature began to become true because by Shiv's grace suddenly that tiger became her devotee. Now it was indeed a changed being, guarding its chosen deity.

Menwhile pleased with Parvati's worship Brahma decided to appear before her. As he asked her to have her desired boon from him, she said she wanted to become again 'Gauri' (or gori) or a fair complexioned female. Brahma granted her the boon.

As she received the boon she started to shed all the dark cells (kosha) off her body and again become fair complexioned. From those dropped dark cells, then, emerged a dark and deadly goddess called Kashiki or Kali.

Endowed with the weapons provided to her by Brahma, Kali killed the two demons Shumbha and Nishumbha in no time, to the great delight of the gods.

Parvati, having achieved her objective, happily returned to her lord, Shiv who smilingly welcomed him as Ghauri again. Shiv, on hearing about that tiger's transformation of nature due to the effect of Parvati's worship, turned the beast into a man and sent him in the employment of Nandi, his 'Gana-chief'. That beast 's name became Somanandi, an able assistant to Nandi.

❑❑

27.
The Tale of Upamanyu

There was a renowned sage Vyagrapada but he was not affluent at all. In fact he was so much poor that he could not afford to give milk to his only son named Upamanyu.

The tale starts when Upamanyu was just a kid. He asked his mother to give him some milk as he was hungry. But the milk given by her mother to him didn't taste like milk. He complained to his mother. "You haven't given me milk but something else in its place. I have tasted milk at my uncle's place. That was real milk. What you have given me was a liquid which did appear like milk but had not that taste. Why did you do so."

His mother canddly admitted: "Dear Son! What I had given to you was the solution of rice pounded and mixed in water. I have no option. We are not as much rich as to provide you a staple diet of milk."

Saying so, Upamanyu's mother began to cry in utter helplessness. But Upamanyu, like a grown up person consoled her: "Don't cry, O Mother, " he requested :"I will pray to Shiv and get milk for myself."

His mother then taught him the 'Mantras' that she had learnt for invoking Shiv's blessing and other details of performing Shiv's worship Lastly she also taught him the way of invoking the deadly weapon 'Aghorastra' in case he felt any danger to his life.

Thus prepared and armed with 'Mantras' and 'Shashtra' Upamanyu left for the Himalayas and started to meditate. He lived only on air and chanted the incantations that his mother had taught him. He had built an earthen linga before which he would pray devoutly for months together. There were disturbance caused by the demons and the beasts but Upamanyu continued his prayers undistracted. Shiv, learning about the devout 'tapasya' that Upamanyu was performing to seek his Darshan, was quite impressed with the boy's tenaucity and Concentration. But he thought to test Upamanyu first. He appeared before him in the guise of Indra and asked : "Upamanyu, What are you doing?"

"Blessed is my life that the king of the gods has appeared before me, replied Upamanyu, delighted at the appearance of the top deity. "I am here praying to Shiv."

"Praying to Shiv !" the deity asked with a show of contempt, "that home-less half-naked wanderer who loses his sense in the addiction of various narcotic drugs?"

Upamanyu was angry at this so derogatory reference to Shiv. He couldn't stand it. So in his uncontrollable anger he immediately summoned the 'Aghorastra' to teach this arrogant king of the gods a lesson. Charging it with the 'mantra' he set it on his bow and shot it towards the deity, disguised as Indra. Seeing this, Indra, who was no one else but Shiv himself with disguise, Came before Upamanyu in his original form. As Shiv appeared there, the 'Aghorastra' was quickly repeled by Nandi who is never away from Shiv. Shiv not only granted the boon that Upamanyu would never have the dearth of milk but also taught him, personally, all sorts of sacred knowledge. Thus, receiveing his desire boon and the assurance of inexhaustible supply of milk, Upamanyu returned home.

Many years later, in Dwaper Age, Krishna had also met the sage Upamanyu. Upamanyu taught him the words of widsom that he had learnt from Shiv. It was by praying Shiv that Krishna obtained his son Sampa. Krishna had prayed to Shiv for sixteen months to get the desired son from Shiv's grace. Parvati also appeared before Krishna to grant him several boons.

❏❏

28.
Andhakasura And Hiranyaksha

S hiv was sitting and quitely mediating on the mount of Mandar. Parvati, in a Jovial mood, came from behind so that Shiv couldn't see her and covered Shiv's eyes with her two hands. Since Shiv couldn't see anything everything appeared dark to him. But while in doing so, Parvati had to exert a bit which made a drop of sweat ooze out and fell down on the ground. From this sweat, a dark and fierce creature was born who started to roar.

Now Shiv was upset. "Parvti ! what are you doing ? Closing my eyes from behind and now roaring ferociously,"

"Its not I, Lord," Parvati said . "See for yourself. This deadly creature. I wonder where did he come form?"

Parvati removed her hands and Shiv saw a horrible creature before him. "It is our son, Parvati" Shiv opined ,"since it was born from sweat when you had kept my eyes covered. Since it was born when I could see nothing but darkeness, let his name be Andhaka."

Andhaka was born blind when his mortal sire could see nothing but darkness. It was adopted by Hiranyaksha or Hiranyanetra, the demon lord, brother of the Hiranyakashyapu of Prahalad's fame[1], In fact Hiranyaksha was more powerful than his brother Hiranyakashyapa, for in his arrogance he had taken the entire earth down to the bottom of the oceans. He had also troubled the gods very severely who prayed Vishnu to come to their help. It was then Vishnu had adopted the form of a huge Varaha (boar), and going down he managed to replace the earth at its proper position after slaying

---

1. The story is too well known to recounted here again

Hiranyaksha. After Hiranyaksha's death, Vishnu made Andhaka the ruler of the empire over which Hiranyaksha had ruled.

When he was crowned as the king, his cousin, Prahlad with other relations, went to him and said : "Brother, you're blind. How can you effectively rule over the kingdom with this handicap. We better advise you to give it to us. Perhaps our uncle committed a blunder by accepting the blind son from Shiv."

Andhaka was cut to the quick hearing these nasty words said by his cousions. He went away straight to the forest and started performing a very difficult penance to please the creator. For uncountable years he kept on standing on his one leg with arm constantly raised heavenwards. It is belived to have been an unprecedented hard tapasya, still uneqalled by any devotee. During his entire tapasya neither he drank a drop of water or ate a morsel of food. In the desperation he had also started chopping his body limbs one by one, offering the chopped parts to the sacred fire. In no time there appeared not even a little flesh left on his body. All his flesh had been cousumed by the holy fire. He had become barely a skeleton when Brahma chose to appear before him.

"What do you want son", said Brahma

"My Cousins Prahlad and others have taken over the kingdom bequeathed to me," began Andhaka: "because I am blind. So give me the first boon: that I may be able to see. If you are happy enough by my devout worship, please deign to grant me another boon : that I may not be killed by the gods, demons or humans-not even by great Vishnu."

Now Brahma was on the thorns of dilemma. "If I allow this boon, he won't be ever killed because the earlier demons who sought similar boons did not mention the name of Vishnu in the best of persons they named to be saved from. With the result, to the Creation's welfare, Vishnu could appear and kill them. But here is a demon who is mentioning Vishnu by name," thought Brahma quietly. He had to find a way out in which the demons' difficult penance might not remain without the due reward, but, at the same time, he might not become immortal."

Then thinking more over it, he said to Andhaka : Deer son ! This is a mortal world. He who is born here must die.

By doing good deeds you only get the right of choosing the conditions of your expiring.

You may tell it and your all other boons shall also be granted." Concluded the creator.

"Since death is ineviteble, "said Andhaka, "let it be under the following conditions. If I ever wish to marry a beautiful woman who is like mother unto me, let it be the moment of my death."

Since this was better that no condition at all, Brahma readily granted the boon. Andhaka, riding a crest of victory, returned to his kingdom. When his cousins learnt about his powers, pulverised, they not only returned Andhaka's empire but added to it their's also out of panic. "Even without eyes he was hardly beatable," thought Prahlad. "Now with the eyes he would be literally invincible by any man, demon or god."

As soon as the domestic disturbances were over, Andhaka attacked heaven. He defeated Indra and other gods, brought heavens under his sway, and made the gods pay heavy taxes to the demon Lord.

Next he attacked and defeated the Naags (snakes), the Gandharvas, the Rakshasas[1], Kubera and his clan of the Yakshas and, of course, humans. Thus he began to rule over all the three worlds with ultimate authority. For immeasurable period Andhaka ruled in this unflattered manner. The holy sculptures including the Vedas were thrown to winds, no Yagyas were allowed and the righteous conduct became the first casualty.

Once Andhaka happened to visit the Mount Mandara. He liked the place so much that he decided to dwell here. He ordered his three lietenants : Duryodhana, Vighasa and Hasti to find a suitable place to dwell. While the three were exploring the environment of Mount Mandar, they hit upon a nice cave. A hermit was sitting inside, busy in his meditation. Dressed in the skin of a tiger and wearing a garland of skulls, that eremite's hair was matted with a gleaning crescent moon shone from his forehead. Sitting close to that eremite was a beautiful woman. She was the combiest woman the lietenants of

---

1. A class or species of the demon having very big body; they were supposed to be the guardians of the wild wealth.

Andhaka had seen in their entire existence. "She ought to be our queen" and with this decision they returned to Andhaka and told all that they had seen. "Then why did you return here empty handed", thumbered Andhaka: "Go back to that eremite and ask him for the woman."

As instructed, Duryodhana, Vighasa and Hasti went back to the eremite who was no one else but Lord Shiv himself and the woman, Parvati. They accosted the eremite : "Well, you are only an ascetic and hence you don't deserve such a beautiful woman as your wife. She ought to be the wife of some king as our master is, He is the Lord of all the three realm and hence immensely rich. He had received boon from Brahma. Give this woman to us so that our master could marry her."

"Ask your master to come here and take the woman himself, " replied the eremite(Shiv).

As soon as the matter was reported to Andhaka he grasped his sword and come to fight with the 'eremite. The door to the cave was guarded by Nandi and hence Andhaka had to first fight with Nandi. Nandi easily defeated the demon and also defeated his soldiers. But a resilient Andhaka soon returned and again a fight ensued beween him and Nandi which lasted for five hundred years. Brahma, Vishnu, Indra and other gods also came there to help Shiv in that battle against Andhaka.

The lietenant of Andhaka, Vighasa was a strong warrier. He opened his mouth wide and swallowed up all the gods including Vishnu. Thus far, Shiv had not actively participated in the war. But hearing that Vighasa had swallowed the gods including his chosen Lord Vishnu, he ascended to the bull, his favourite mount, and came out challenging the demon for a dwell. He killed Vighesa and rescued the gods from the demon's stomach.

Now, the asura (demons) had a preceptor named Shukracharya who knew the art of reviving the dead being to life with the help of a formula called " Mrita-sanjivan". So the demons requested him and he began to revive back to life the slain demon-hosts. The gods panicked. They again prayed Shiv to end this phenomenon. Shiv then ordered his Ganas (hench-persons) to catch hold of Shukracharya and as he was brought before him, he swallowed the demon-guru.

Then all demons were destroyed except Andhaka. He continued to fight. Even Vishnu's famous mace 'Kaumudi' couldn't check his violent onslaughts. Even Indra's Vajra or thunder bolt could do little to check the dreadful demon's advance. All the gods' weapons could only hurt the demon, causing some blood drops to emerge from his wounds. But as the drops of blood fell to the ground they created a fresh Andhaka. As a result, the battle field appeared to be filled up with uncountable number of Andhakas. There were millions of Andhaka.

In order to fight this Maya-Yuddha' (illusive war) against the demon-lord, Shiv created a Goddess called Devi. This fearsome female existence was created by Shiv from his own body, Shiv asked the Devi to drink up the blood of the demon that was falling on to the battle field and creating new Andhaka. Thus helped by the Devi, Shiv started to tackle the demons and soon all were slain, barring the original Andhaka. Seeing just before him Shiv hurled his trident at him which struck Andhaka on the Chest and instantly killed him.

The war, now, was over and the gods chanted hymns in the glory of Lord Shiv. Then at the request of the surviving demons, Shukracharya, the demons guru was released by Shiv through his urinary track. Hence semen also came to be known as 'Shukra'. Thus the demon Andhaka was destroyed and peaec and Vaidic order returned to all the three realms.

❏❏

29.
The Story Of Ruru

There was yet another demon who wanted to have Parvati as his wife. His name was Ruru. Once while roaming on the mountains he happened to see Parvati. He was so enamoured of her beauty that he decided then and there to have Parvati as his wife. With this resolve he went to perform 'tapasya' to please Brahma so that he might seek the boon from the Creator to grant Parvati as his wife.

In due time Brahma appeared before him and asked : "Ruru ! Why are you performing such a difficult tapasya. What is that you are aiming at ?"

"Make Parvati my wife," requested Ruru.

"That is the boon I seek from you as a consequence of my worship to you."

"This isn't a boon that even I can not possibly grant to you, no matter how devout be your worship. Ask for something else." Brahma said.

But Ruru insisted on having only that boon. Since it was beyond Brahma's powers, the creator went back and Ruru continued with his meditation making it all the more deep.

Ruru was doing this meditation worship at a mountain called Malaya. Ruru had started making it so intense that due to the heat generated by it, even the mountain range began to burn. It soon developed such far reaching leaping flames that even Shiv who was staying close by with Parvati had to run away to a safe place.

Parvati was amazed : "Lord why are we running away ? Why don't you try to douse these flames with your yogic powers."

"I can't " said Shiv: "These flames are being caused by Ruru's intense 'tapasya' in order to obtain you as his wife. So it is upto you to do whatever you decide about these flames."

Getting the real reason, Parvati decided to do something about it. While Shiv and Parvati were discussing the issue, Parvati happened to spot a lion fighting with an elephant. Parvati or Uma immediately slew the lion and skinned it to don the lion's skin as her clothing. Owing to the blood oozing out from the skin her hair became smeared with the lion's blood, making her look terrible in appearance.

Then she bellowed loudly and rushed to where Ruru was.

"Ruru ! Recognise me ? I am Parvati. I am the one," Parvati said : "For Whom you have been praying so devoutly. I am here now. Stop meditating",

"Don't talk nonsense," Ruru blurted : "You can't be Parvati. She is the most beautiful woman in the world. And you...... you look terrible and repulsive. While she is like the moon and her complexion aureate, you are dark and ugly. While her arms like the lotus stem, your arms look sturdy and uncomely. You cann't be Parvati. I tell you-you quit before I take my rash action. I don't want you."

Saying so, Ruru struck Parvati with a mace. Enraged at the demon's temerity, she hit Ruru with her fists. Then a fierce fight ensued between them. Ruru kept flinging at her boulders and trees while she used her nails and teeth to trounce the demon. Ruru, through his black magical powers created several demons which pounced on Parvati. In retaliation Parvati made several Shakti's (powers) appear from her body which began to gobble up the demons created by Ruru.

Seeing his forces weakening in the combat, Ruru fled and Parvati persued him to the ends of the earth. To avoid her, he fled to heaven but Parvati followed him. Then he fled to Patal (neither world) but Parvati also reached there. Finally there was no place left for Ruru to escape to. Then Parvati caught hold of him and tore of his head with her bare nails. Seeing her adversary dead, Parvati roared and drank his blood. Then she skinned the demon with her hands and took the pelt with her.

Thus killing Ruru, Parvati returned to Shiv. Parvati gave him the lion's skin as a present. It was the same skin wearing which Parvati had killed Ruru. Shiv gratefully donned it. And Parvati attired herself in the skin of Ruru. That is the form Parvati is worshipped as the nemesis of all the demon's and evil person.

❑❑

30.
Appearance of A False Parvati

Once Shiv with his entourage left for a city called Shonitpur, leaving Parvati behind. He was accompanied by many Gandharvas and Apsaras [divine musicians and dancers]. But soon he started missing Parvati. Shiv summoned Nandi and asked him to go and fetch Parvati.

Nandi dutifully repaired to Kailash and told Parvati: "Mother! The Lord wants you near him. You must accompany me. I will take you to him."

But Parvati was not ready to leave in such a short notice. She said : "Nandi ! You go back and tell him that I cannot leave immediately. I need some time to prepare for the journey."

Nandi went back and gave Shiv the message from Parvati. Shiv waited for some time but Parvati didn't come He, therefore, again asked Nandi to go to Kailash and return withParvati and her companions pronto.

As Nandi went, the Apsaras and the Gandharvas, detecting Shiv's impatience to have Parvati with him, decided to play a practical joke. They created a false Parvati, false Nandi and Parvati's other companions with such an aplomb that even Shiv failed to recognise a false Parvati and Nandi While Shiv with his henchpersons, the Apsaras and the Gandharvas, was having great fun with that false Parvati without recognising the reality, lo and behold ! There also reached the real Parvati, her true companions with the real Nandi. This created a massive confusion as each party called itself to be the real group. At last, having great fun at Shiv's cost, the Apsaras adopted their real

110

form. They apologised for the 'play' and said : "Blessed is that Devi Parvati who is such a beloved of her husband. May she be a model for every married woman" !

Shiv and Parvati both enjoyed the 'play' without minding it the least. They, on the contrary, praised the Apsaras and the Gandharvas for playing the deception with such perfection. Then the Apsaras and the Gandharvas went to their realm and Shiv with Parvati, Nandi and other henchpersons left for Kailash, their eternal abode.

❑❑

31.
Yet Another False Parvati

As mentioned earlier, once Parvati was addressed as 'Kali' and in anger she had gone away to become fair again. But before her going, remembering her Lord Shiv's penchant for narcoatic drugs and then not recognising even his wife as happened when the Gandharvas and Apsaras played a trick on him, she called Nandi aside and said: "Nandi ! You know Your Lord ! He does not know the difference between real Parvati and the pseudo one. So keep a watchful guard at the gate and don't let any false Parvati dare enter the place." With this express intention she departed to the jungles to perform her 'tapasya' to become fair again.

During that period there was an Asura (demon) called Adhi. He had performed a very difficult penance to please Brahma. When the deity appeared he desired a boon of immortality from him. Brahma said : " Sorry! In this mortal world everyone who is born must die some day. This is the rule of Nature and cannot be disturbed. You may have some other boon from me."

"Then make me the strongest person on the earth," Adhi requested. This boon Brahma granted readily. He also gave him the boon to adopt any form. Armed with this boon the demon wandered around in the Himalaya. He happened to reach near Kailash as well. There he found Nandi guarding the abode of Shiv.

"What are you doing here ?" the demon asked Nandi.

Nandi told all that Parvati had instructed him about. He didn't hide anything deeming the demon to be an ascetic.

The demon, learning about Shiv's this weakness hatched a conspiracy. He immediately disguised himself as Parvati. Fearing that Nandi may recognise him in the disguised form, the wicked demon chose the form of a tiny snake and managed to pass himself through the tiny cave at the gate undetected. Reaching inside Shiv's chamber, he adopted the form of Parvati. Then he went to meet Shiv who couldn't see through the demon's game and came ahead enthusiastically to welcome his wife. But no sooner than Shiv took the false Parvati into his arms-fold that the demon appeared in his true guise. Then he tried to kill Shiv. The moment Shiv realised who his opponent was, he fought with him and a bloody duel ensued. Soon the demon was slayed by Shiv. But before dying the wicked played another trick on Shiv and said : "I have a brother who looks like me but he is stronger than me. Soon he will be coming again disguised as Parvati to kill you." It was only a false alarm raised by the demon as he had no brother. But he did so to confuse Shiv. Then he died.

However the demon's trick worked. As soon as Parvati returned completing her 'tapasya' and regaining her real complexion, Shiv thought her to be the slain demon's brother in disguise, and a bloody war started between the husband and wife. Shiv created many beings from his body to kill Parvati. In retaliation Parvati also created many Shaktis from her body after having failed to convince her husband of her real existance. Soon the Shaktis created by Parvati swallowed the beings created by Shiv. It was only then that Shiv realised his mistake, for no other being could have generated as many Shaktis as to swallow up the beings created by Lord Shiv. Realising his mistake he embraced Parvati and all was well in Kailash.

❏❏

32

Two Illustrious Guests of Yama

There were four psychic sons of Brahma. Their names were Sanaka, Sanatan, Sanandan and Sanata kumar. They were all very learned. By Brahma's one boon they ever remain in Child-form. One of them, Sanat kumar had once visited Yama-lok (Yama, the death god's realm) to over see the arrangement there on the advice of Brahma. While Santakumar was holding a discussion with Yama, he spotted a 'Vimana' (the divine flying vehicle) landing in the yama's realm. Out emerged from the shining viman an illustrious person before whom Yama bowed very reverentially and asked : " Did you feel any inconvience, Sir ? I'm honoured by your presence in my realm ." After worshipping' the person devoutly Yama said : "This vimana shall now take you to Brahma's realm where you have earned a place due to your numerous Punyas (religious merits). Thanks for visiting my realms."

Then Yama guided that Vimana to its decided destination. After the exit of this guest, shortly there arrived another guest in yet another shining vimana who was also accorded the same reverential treatment as was shown to the first guest. After giving this vimana also to its decided destination with full respect and veneration, Yama returned to Sanatakumar. Now, this child sage was quite mystified.

"Who could be these two persons who were accorded such reverential treatment by Yama, the death-god himself. This sort of treatment is reserved only to the Super gods viz Brahma, Vishnu and Mahesh? Who could they be?" When Sanatakumar persisted with these questions, Yama obliged by telling details about these two nobel souls.

There was a city named Vidisha. The king who ruled there was Dharapala. He was quite a noble king. Once he visited the jungle for hunting. There he found a jackal performing a devout worship to Shiv.

Since Dharapala was a noble king he learnt by his yogic powers all about this jackal. That Jackal was no other but Nandi, passing a period of the curse Parvati had charged him with. His fault was that he had allowed the false Parvati's entry into Shiv's chamber. [The story had been already given in details].

Parvati had cursed Nandi for this lapse that for twelve years he would have to pass his life in the form of a jackal.

The jackal then went straight to the rivers Vitasta and Vetravati. There it sat up a linga and prayed before it, going without any food or water. After the expiry of the twelve year's period, the jackal died and his soul adopting a shining form went back to the realm of Shiv as Nandi.

It was to this jackal that the king, Dharapala had observed doing a divout penance He also witnessed his strange death. The king was wonder-struck. "Can a jackal also attain to the realm of Shiv by his devout worship of the linga." he thought. But having seen the spectacle he also had a linga created in a wonderful temple close to the confluence of the rivers. He brought some brahmanas to the temple and made then recite the holy Puranas and other scriptures non-stop. This noble act accumulated a huge religious merit for the king when he died. It was ordained that he would go to Brahma's realm because of his stored 'Punyas'. It was his soul which had arrived in the death-god, Yama's domain and which received such a severential welcomes there.

"And who was the other guest ?" asked Sanata kumar having heard about the first guest. Yama then told him the details about the second guest.

The second guest was no god-realised soul. It was, in fact, an evil person engaged in the wicked acts. But once trapped in a lonely spot, he was forced to listen the narration of the holy Puranas which totally changed him. He became a devout, god-fearing and noble person. Then, he arranged many recitals of the Puranas and the holy texts on his own and donated gold to the Brahmanas and noble persons.

His later acts earned huge 'Punyas' for him, enough to take him to the realm of Brahma. The holy scriptues reveal that the one who gets converted into a noble person from being wicked gets his Punya in double measure. Such are the rewards of listening to the recitation of the holy Puranas which allow even wicked to go to heaven. Listening to the holy Puranas is as good as worshipping the Holy trinity (Brahma, Vishnu, Mahesh) will full faith.

□□

33.

The Story of Shatanika And Sahastranika

Continuing the narration, Romaharshan told the assembled gathering about this story of Shatanika and Sahastranika.

Eons ago there dwelled in the region called Jambudweepa[1], a noble king named Shatanika. He was not only a renowned warrior but a very righteous person. Everyday he donated huge alms to the brahmanas. He aso treated his guests with great honour. Having lived upto full age the king died. His son called Sahastranika ascended to the throne.

Although Sahastranika was also a very noble king he did not devote as much alms to the brahmanas as his father used to do. The brahmanas were unhappy on this account and one day, they came in a delegation to register their complaint with the king. "You give us much less gold and other things then what we were receiving from your father. This pauciaty in alms has forced many noble brahmanas leave your kingdom. Many more will follow them if you don't enhance the quantum of the alms you give to us."

But Sahastranika was not affected by their complaints.

He said: "Of course, I know that alms given to brahmana results in the accumulation of 'Punya' in a large measure to donor and ensures the donor's birth in heaven. But I am curious to know where my father has actually gone after giving so many alms to the brahmanas. Since you all are noble brahmanas with whole of universe accessible to you, you must tell me the final state my father's soul resting in.

---

1. The Indian peninsula, named so because of the abundance of Jamun trees—called 'Jambu' in Sanskrit.

Please find out this and only then I would be convinced of the merit accruing to the donor by giving huge alms. Will you do it for me?."

The delegation of the brahmanas kept quiet. They had no idea where king Shatanika's soul might be resting. While they were brooding over as to know about the died king's soul, they happened to meet a learned sage, named Bhargava. He was quite powerful and had vast yogic powers at his command. The brahmanas were sure that sage Bhargava would be able to tell about the wherebouts of the died king Shatanika.

The sage was hardly interested in involving himself in the task of knowing as to where the died king's soul was resting, He knew that one gets good or bad realms in accordance with the noble or bad deeds performed in life. But the brahmanas kept on requesting him about this job and reluctantly he agreed. Then the sage prayed to the sun-god who led him, to the abode of Yama, the ultimate authority to decide where a soul should go.

In that realm the Sun-god first led the sage to the twenty eight crores of naraka (halls). The wailings of the sinners could be clearly heard who were being tortured on account of their performing evil deeds. But before the sage could go any further, his way was barred by a brahmana.

"O sage," the mysterious brahmana said : "You owe me a gold coin for the services I rendered for your cause. You couldn't square the account during my life time. Now you must pay it before you move any further in this realm."

"But I don't have any coin on my person to settle the account," replied Bhargava. "Settle it when I return. I will get a coin from Yama to settle the account. But now let me move forward," the sage said.

"In this realm there is no credit and all accounts are to be settled in hard cash.

There is no provision for making the payment later. In any case, if you don't have any money on your person, then I would be happy to settle the account provided you part with one sixth of the entire Punya that you have accumulated so far through your meditations and worship."

Bhargava had to settle for this, and then he moved further ahead. He was, successively stopped by a cowherd, a washerman, a tailor, a priest and a builder. To each of them he owed some money and they would not let him move further till the debt was cleared. To all of them he had to give one sixth of the 'punya' that had accumulated to his credit.

At last, led by the Sun-god, Bhargava managed to reach before a tub having a person, boiled in oil. Recognising the person Bhargava was bewildered. "How come the king Shatanika is being tortured so cruelly? He was a noble king? Having lots of 'punya' to his name owing to the large amounts of gold and other things he donated as alms ! Was he not righteous or a 'Punya'-shali' (a person with lots of religious merit)?"

The soul of the king Shatanika heard Bhargava and said : "No doubt, I used to donate huge alms but not from my earnings. The money had come from the royal treasury. So the merit for doing so has been credited to the people's account. You better go and tell my son that 'Punya' as best accumulates by associating with noble persons and donating alms earned out of your earnings. Tell him to do so while reverenteally offering all the merits to the Blessed Lord Shiv. Pray to him everyday, particularly on every 14 th day of the lunar fortnight. Only then he could redeem me from this hell and ensure for himself a nook in the heaven."

Returning to Jamabudweep, Bhargava told Sahastrinika all that the lettter's departed father had advised him to convey to him, Sahasteamika got the message. Now he started donating alms for which he earned money by himself toiling hard as a labourer after his royal duties.

He also religiously prayed Shiv and observed a strict fast on the Fourteenth day of every lunar fortnight. This practice not only rebarred his father's soul from the tortures of hell but also made him earn a sure birth in heaven. One shouldn't donate anything as alms which has not been earned by his personal merit. At last both the son and the father earned a place in Shiv-loka (Shiv's realm).

❑❑

34.
Parashuram's Story

Long ago there was a renowned king named Gadhi. His daughter was married to a sage Richuka who was an especialist in performing sacrifices.

Once Richuka arranged for a very pious sacrifice which resulted in his receiving some divine potion (Khura) from the holy fire. Richuka gave that khura to his wife Satyavati with the instructions. "I would divide this divine potion in to two portions. Eat first half yourself and the remaining half should be eaten by your mother." Then the sage divided himself the potion into even parts and gave them to his wife to have it consumed according to the precise instructions already given. He also explained the purpose of dividing the divine potion. "Since we are brahmanas living in a hermitage, we need a son with virtuous qualities of a brahmana. But your father as a 'kshatriya' (of mortal race)," he said : "needing a robust son with a warrior like qualities. So your (first) part should give you a noble brahmana while the other part, a noble kshatriya."

Yet despite these clear instructions the mother and the daughter interchanged the parts. Meanwhile Richuka had left for the woods to continue with his meditation. While doing so he realised the mistake her wife and his mother-in-low had committed through his especial powers. Through his powers he managed to postpone the birth of his son. So, Satyawati eventually gave birth to Jamadagni. It was Jamadagni's son, Parashurama, who exhibited the Kshatriya-like qualities despite being a brahman.

And eventually Gadhi's son became Vishwamitra. He was a born Kshatriya but by meditation and penance he could attain the highest position achievable by a brahmana : Brahamarishi' (the Supreme Sage)

Jamdagni subsequently got more sons as well. Once his wife Renuka delayed in preparing things for his worship. He became so angry that he asked his sons to behead their mother for this lapse. None except Parshuram came forward to do so after ensuring a desired boon from his father following his carrying out the latter's order. In no time he beheaded his mother and by virtue of his boon he received from his father he could revive his mother back to life.

Parashuram's real name was Ram. But since he always carried an axe he came to be known as the Ram with the axe.

When Parashuram came of age, there was a renowned king of the Hailaya Dynasty named Arjuna . He had also obtained the boon that flaming fire itself would be perpetually present on the tip of his arrow. Whenever he shot an arrow that became an arrow with raging fire. This way Arjuna used to burn up villages and forests.

Once in his arrogance he dared to burn the hermitage of a saint who cursed him that he would be slain by Parashuram.

Meanwhile Parashuram, as was destined, became a master in weilding weapons. He learnt the art of fighting from no one else but Lord Shiv himself. Once Arjuna happened to arrive at Jamadagni's hermitage. Jamadagni offered his whole entourage the choicest food and other things of comfort. The king Arjuna asked the sage as to how could he arrange so much of food and other things for his men in that thick jungle, that too, in no time. The sage Jamadagni replied that it was all due to a divine cow (Kamadhenu) which he had. "She would give whatever you want."

Going greedy for such a fabulous cow, Arjuna, the king, asked Jamadgni to give that cow to him but the sage refused to oblige the king. Where upon the king, Arjuna, ordered his sepoys to forcibly take the cow. But as they were about to do so, there arrived Parashuram, with his axe. He killed the king, believed to be having a thousand arms, slicing all the arms and made the soldiers of the king flee in panic.

Having killed Arjuna, Parashurama went off to his meditation and worship of Lord Shiv. Taking the advantage of Parashurama's absence, the sons of Arjuna collected a huge army and attacked the sage 'Jamadagni's hermitage. In looting the hermitage they also killed the sage Jamadgni. When Parashuram returned from Mahendra Parvata, his favourite spot for worship, he exacted the revenge for this evil deed and killed Arjuna's all sons, thus extrcminating the entire dynasty. Then he developed a great vengeance for the entire Kshatriya race and twenty one time he almost made the Kshatriyas extinct from the surface of the earth. He did so for twenty one times because the sons of Arjuna had inflicted twenty one wounds on Jamadgni's body before finally killing him.

But while doing so Parashurama committed a heinous crime of murder. As penance he had to donate thousands of well-bedecked cows and perform many yagyas including the top one, 'Ashwamedha'[horse's sacrifice] .

But this was found to be not adequate penance. Then he sought advice from the Primal sage Kashyapa who advised him to perform Tuladana regularly after offering oblation to Lord Shiv. Tuledana is a special type of alms giving act in which the person weights himself against the gold, honey, clarified butter and other holy items to be given as alms, and donates the weighed things to the needy brahmanas. With this he was absolved of the sin and then he repaired to Mahendra Parvata to continue his worship to Lord Shiv, his chosen deity and master. He is believed to be age less and hence he keeps on appearing in every age. He was present at Rama's time when he had an altercation with Rama when the latter broke Shiv's Bow to win Sita's hand in marriage.

He was also present during the time Mahabharata was fought since he is described to be the guru of Karna in archery.

❑❑

35.

Description of Hells, Geography, Astronomy, Time Division And Menns

This Purana, like the other Purana describes about several halls. These hells infect, are the punishment meted out to various sinners like the 'Tapta loha' which literally means the sinner is forced to sit on red-hot iron. Their names or punishments for the offence are given below.

(i) Raurava:- A killer of Brahmana's; One who gives false witness; a liar; a drinker of prohibitive drinks including liquor are consigned to it.

(ii) Shookara:- For killer of cattle and thieves. The killers of the Kshatriyas and the Vaishya are also sent here.

(iii) Taptaloha:- For those who commit infanticide (slaying the infants)

(iv) Tapta Bhala:- For those who criticise their teachers and the Vedic texts.

(v) Krimibhaksha: Those who insult the brahmanas, gods, or kings are consigned to this hell.

(vi) Lalabhaksha : For those who eat without offering obtain to the gods and for the brahmanas who eat prohibited things.

(vii) Rudhirandha: For the sellers of liquor and for those who kill hapless beings.

(viii) Vaitarani: For killers of Bees.

(ix) Asipatravana : For the destroyer of trees and vegetation.

(x) Krishna : For the Cheats.

(xi) Vahnijwala: For the killers of mute animals.

(xii) Agnimaya : For those who cause destruction by fire.

(xiii) Sandamsha: Those who fail to complete their Varata or fulfill their commitment.

(xiv) Shvabhojana : For those who follow their sons' instructions.

Although punishment is quite proportional to the crime or sin committed, one can dilute one's sin by atoning for it through penance. The best way to get redemption for the most heinous crime or sin is to worship Shiv.

Geography

According to this Purana the earth is divided into seven main continents (dweepas) : Jamabudweepa, Plakshadweep, Shalmalidweep, Shakadweepa, Kushadweep, Kronchdweepa and Pushkardweepa. These main regions are surrounded by seven Oceans which are Lavana, Ikshu, Sanpi, Dahi, Dugdha, Jala and Rasa[1] [As is apparent, Lavana means salty, Ikshu means sour, sanpi means bitter, Dahi means curds, Dugdha means milk, Jala means water and Rasa means juice].

Mount Sumeru is described to be located right in the middle of Jambudweepa. This centre portion of Jambudweep is called Ilavritavarsha. To the south of Sumeru is Bharatavarsha, to the north is Ramyakavasha and further north is Uttarakuruvarsha. Bharat varsha is bounded by mountain ranges in the north and the sea on the south. Seven main mountain ranges of Bhartavarsha are Mahendra, Malaya, Sahya, Shuktimana, Riksha, Vindhya and Partyatra.

Bharatavarsha is a sacred place. Only those who have accumulated 'Punya' over a thousand human lives get to be born in Bharatavarasha since Shiv is always present here to provide salvation to its dwellers.[1]

Astronomy

The boundaries of the Bhuloka (earth) extend upto the points that can be hit up by the rays of the Sun and the Moon. Above the

---

1. These Ocean represent the fluids that were popular in those times; they also give an impression of the tastes that were known that time.

2. Since most of these details have already been given in 'The Vishnu Purana' of our this series, they are being given here only briefly.

region of the Sun is that of the Moon. Then after there are the realms of Buddha (Mercury), Shukra(Venus), Mangala(Mars), Brihaspati (Jupiter), Shani(Seturn), and that of the nakshatras (constellations). After this spreads the realm of Saptarishi loke (the constellation of the Ursa Majoris). Beyond them is Swargaloka (heaven). During the Pralaya only Bhuloka, Bhuvarloka and Swargaloka are destroyed but not the realms beyond. The first, beyond these three is Dhruvloka, the circle of the Pole Star. So the seven (realms) are Bhuloka, Bhuvarloka, Swargaloka, Dhruvaloka, Maharloka, Janloka, Tapalokaand Satyaloka. The underworld is Patalloka whose seven divisions are Patala, Sutala, Vetala, Nitala, Mahatala, Agryasutalaand the lowest is Rasatala.

Time Division And the Manvantaras

Nimesha is the smallest unit of time which is equivallent to time taken in blinking eyes once.

15 Nimeshas = 1 Kashtha; 30 Kashtha = 1 Kala; 30 Kala = One Muhurta and 30 Muhurta = 1 Day; 30 Days = 1 month which has two lunar fortnights (bright and dark)

Shuklapaksha and Krishnapaksha. 6 months = 1 Ayana, thus 2 Ayana = 1 years; 360 human years = 1 divine year. Satyayuga=4000 Divine years, Treta yuga=3000 divine years, Dwaper yuga = 2000. Divine years, Kaliyga = 1000 Divine year. The Sandyas and Sandhyamsha, the intervening period between the onset of one Yug, account for 2000 divine years- thus one cycle of four Yugas = 12000 divine Years, 1 Kalpa=1000 cycles of the four Yugas =14 Manvantaras, the long period in which one Manu of rules. 1 Kalpa= 1Day of Brahma ; 3000 Brahma Years = Yuga a Brahma 1000 Such Yugas = 1 Savana and one Brahma lives for three thousand Savauas. During each of Vishnu's Days one Brahma is born and dies and during each of Shiv's days one Vishnu is born and dies.

As mentioned before each Manvantra is ruled by one Manu. The gods (devatas) the seven great sages and Indra change from one Manavantara to another.

The first Manu was Swayambhuva and the names of the seven sages were Mareechi, Atri, Angira, Pulastya, Pulaha, Kratu and Vashishtha. This way the Manus, Indra and the seven Sages keep on changing in every Manvantara. This Purana claims that seven Manvantara of this kalpa have taken place and the remaining seven will come in the future[1] The last(7th) Manu was Vaivaswata.

Vaivasvata Manu

Upon being asked by the sages Romaharshana gave the detailed account of this Manu.

The sage Kashyapa's son was Viswavana or the Sun. The Sun was married to Twastha's (same as Vishkarma) daughter Sangya and they had three children, Vaiveswata, Yama and Yamuna.

When Sangya could not stand the brilliance of her husband, she created her own copy, Sandhya, from her body, and went to live with her father. Meanwhile, the sun couldn't detect the difference and produced yet another son from this union called Saverni.

Since Sandhya doted more on Sararni, neglecting Yama and other issues of the Sun form the first union, the Sun learnt about this difference. Then he went to Twashtha in whose house Sangya was living. But her father had detected her leaving her husband. On being asked why, in anger, she went to the kingdom called Uttaraketu adopting the mare's form. Having learnt the reason of his first wife deserting him, the Sun also followed it to the Uttaraketu kingdom in the form of a horse. Then, as horse and mare they had two children, called the Ashwini kumars. They were also called Nasatya and Dasara. This way Vaivasvata Manu was the son of the Sun and Sangya. He performed many yagya in order to have a son. From this yagya he got a daughter called Ila.

Chandra's (moon's) son Budha(Murcury) married Ila and they had a son named Pururva. This was the origin of the lunar dynasty which started with Pururva who, later on, married to the famous danseuse Urvashi.

Later on, Vaivasvata Manu had nine sons. Their names were Ikshvaku, Shivi, Nabhaga, Dhrishnu, Sharyati, Narishyanta, Isha, Karusha and Priyaverta. These nine sons are believed to be the originators of the solar dynasty. In fact the whole of creation is created by these two principal dynasties.

□□

---

1. Then the Purana mentions about the names of Manus and the seven sages of the coming manvantras

36.
Epilogue

The sages that assembled to listen from Romaharshana the Shiv Purana were quite gratified at its conclusion. They were so thrilled that they worshipped Romaharshana. But Romaharshana warned them: "Never reveal anything about this Purana to those who don't have faith in Shiv or other gods. This Purana deserves to be told to those who are righteous, god-fearing and noble by nature"

One who reads or listens to this Purana's narration becomes a staunch devotee of Shiv. Then he has his all sins automatically washed away. The attentive listener to this Purana receives grace direct from the Lord of Universe, Shiv. One must not only keep this Purana but should also donate it to the deserving ones along with gold and other alms to earn a sure niche in the realm of Shiv.

—:: *OM NAMAH SHIVAYA* ::—

———— ❖❖❖ ————

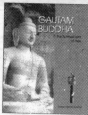
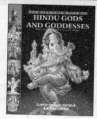

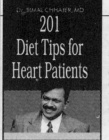